324.22
V244b

THE BIG BOSSES

THE BIG BOSSES

By Charles W. Van Devander

HOWELL, SOSKIN, PUBLISHERS

1944

Copyright, 1944, by Charles Van Devander

TABLE OF CONTENTS

INTRODUCTION

A MERICAN political machines grind out mayors, judges, state legislators and congressmen without much direct control by the voters. In some cities they enable a single Boss, or perhaps two or three insiders, to exercise dictatorial control over all phases of the municipal government and to wield a dominant influence in the selection of state governors and members of the Senate.

But the influence of the Boss on election day can easily be exaggerated. Most voters, even members of strong machines, form their own judgments on the rival candidates for president, governor or mayor. And, thanks to the secret ballot, most of them are able to vote as they choose without fear of retaliation.

The most important part of the machine's work is completed, however, long before election day. The Boss's chief interest always is directed at the primaries or conventions where party control is established and maintained and where the candidates for office are nominated. The Boss can, and frequently does, determine which way the state's votes will be thrown in the National Convention which picks the party candidate for president.

Essentially, every political machine is more concerned with the election of the mayor, sheriff and county judge than it is with the election of a president. It is control of the local offices which provides the patronage which is the life blood of the machine. Naturally, the Boss seeks the nomination of the presidential candidate who will provide the most strength for his local ticket. The influence and the ramifications of the local machines and local bosses in state and national politics are consequently far-reaching.

Who are the Bosses? Which are the chief political machines? How do they operate? Who or what interests support them and benefit from their control of governments? How strong are they, actually?

It is the purpose of this book to answer these questions both from the historical viewpoint, tracing the origins and growth of some of the political machines, and from the viewpoint of present day politics.

1

MURPHY'S SPAWN

I T WAS A BLACK DAY for Tammany Hall when they buried Charles Francis Murphy.

Around the grave on April 28, 1924, foregathered one of the gaudiest collections of silk hats and frock coats New York has ever seen. Notable in the solemn crowd were Governor Alfred E. Smith, Supreme Court Justice and Senator-to-be Robert F. Wagner and Royal S. Copeland, Major John F. Hylan, and State Senator James J. Walker. Each of these owed his political existence to Boss Murphy.

Hundreds of other silk-hatted mourners included the whole state and city judiciary, congressmen, city commissioners and lesser office-holders. And behind the police lines were thousands of just plain people. Many of them were weeping sincerely.

Ten years later "Jimmy" Walker stood beside

Murphy's grave and summed up in one sentence a lurid decade's political history of New York City.

"There," said Walker, "lies all that is left of the brains of Tammany Hall."

Many a discontented member of the New York County Democratic organization has echoed Walker's heart-felt sentiments during the second decade since that day when they laid Murphy and the brains of Tammany to rest.

For twenty-two years—1902 to 1924—Murphy had ruled Tammany as undisputed boss. During most of that period he had been the actual ruler of New York City and, at times, of the state. He had spoken with an influential voice in the national councils of the Democratic Party, and he had, in Al Smith, a strong Tammany candidate for the presidency. A former saloon keeper, with no formal education, he nevertheless had exceptional qualities of political leadership. He steered Tammany through scores of big and little storms and he left, at his death, a spreading political empire and a personal fortune of two million dollars.

Today, what was Murphy's great political realm resembles the ruins of Mussolini's Twentieth Century Roman Empire.

The strong Brooklyn Democratic machine, with which Murphy always maintained a firm alliance, has long since cut itself completely free from Tam-

many. So has the Bronx organization run by Boss
Edward J. Flynn, a Murphy satellite and protege.
Kelly and Flynn can and do dominate the city-
wide decisions of the Democratic Party, as they
showed by nominating a mayoralty candidate opposed by Tammany in the 1937 Democratic primary.

The Tammany Tiger, harried by a succession of
crusading, or merely ambitious, prosecutors; shut
off from its chief sources of patronage by Mayor
LaGuardia in City Hall and Governor Thomas E.
Dewey at Albany; thoroughly discredited by repeated and convincing disclosures of its dominance
by the criminal underworld, has been cornered and
hemmed in no less by its former allies than by its
old foes. Its once fearsome roar is now only a
frightened yelp.

The most recently heard yelping of the Tammany cub resulted from a telephone call made by
City Magistrate Thomas A. Aurelio to a slot-
machine racketeer, Frank Costello, in which the
magistrate gratefully pledged undying loyalty to
Costello for his help in obtaining a Supreme Court
judgeship nomination. The type of scandal which
resulted from this revelation was not new in the
history of Tammany Hall; nor were the pious
gestures of reform and the protestations of innocence particularly novel in Tammany's career.

But in order to understand the significance of

this newest of malodorous chapters in the story of New York City Democracy, it is necessary to know the historical background and the structural organization of Tammany.

Tammany Hall is almost entirely an extra-legal body, superimposed on the regular Democratic Party organization in New York County (Manhattan). But it is so inextricably involved with the legal party machinery that they can be differentiated only by very fine distinctions. Tammany is recognized as the party organization in Manhattan and, in fact, it completely controls all of the party's legal machinery. A brief description of the organization is necessary to provide an understanding of this relationship.

The legal party organization is based on the New York County Democratic Committee, which consists of several thousand members (the number varies) who are elected for two-year terms in election district (voting precinct) units by the enrolled Democrats voting in the party primaries. The County Committee meets soon after each biennial primary and elects a chairman and other officers. The county committeemen elected in each of the twenty-three Assembly districts meet about the same time and organize the Assembly district committee, also headed by a chairman. At the same time the committeemen elect a Tammany district leader and a woman co-leader in each district. Some of the Assembly districts are split for purposes of leadership into two or three parts, so that instead of twenty-three, there are thirty-five district leaders and an equal number of women co-leaders.

The Tammany district leader is the political boss of his district, or portion of a district. The man chosen as chairman of the County Committee for the district always is one of the leader's trusted henchmen, and is purely a figurehead. The woman co-leader also is picked by the leader for her personal loyalty to him. Similarly, the county committeemen themselves are designated by the leader (or successful candidate for leadership) to run in the primary, and they, too, are the district leader's faithful adherents. They are also the active party workers and canvassers, and are rewarded by appointment to serve on local election boards during registration week and on election day, and by other favors at the disposal of the district leader. The Assembly district leader thus is complete czar of the party in his district.

The thirty-five district leaders, with their co-leaders, make up the Executive Committee of the New York County Democratic Committee. As such they are recognized in the New York election law as the guiding body of the Democratic Party between meetings of the full County Committee.

In practice such meetings are rare, and are strictly routine.

The Tammany Executive Committee elects the leader of Tammany Hall, an official who has no party standing at all under the law, but who becomes, in fact, the Democratic county boss. As long as he remains in office he makes all final decisions. He can be overruled by a vote of the Executive Committee, but he rarely is. If a leader should become weak enough to lose control over the committee to that extent, he would almost immediately be deposed.

The leader has the final voice in the designation of Tammany candidates for the Supreme Court, the Court of General Sessions (the County court), and for county and borough (of Manhattan) officials, such as district attorney and borough president. He advises with the district leaders involved, in the designation of candidates for Congress, the State Senate, and the Municipal Court bench, all of whom are elected from districts including more than one Assembly district. And he sits with the county leaders of Kings (Brooklyn), the Bronx, Queens, and Richmond (Staten Island) in selecting the organization designees to run for the party nominations for city-wide offices — mayor, controller, and president of the City Council.

Thus the Tammany system is a boss system from top to bottom. The district leaders are absolute bosses in their districts, and the Tammany Hall leader is the big boss. That is the theory. Much of Tammany's trouble in recent years has been due to the fact that it has a boss system, but has had no man big enough to act as a real boss.

It was John F. Curry who, to paraphrase a Churchillism, presided over the dismemberment and downfall of the Tammany empire.

"Judge" George W. Olvany, who succeeded Murphy as leader, provided a striking demonstration of Tammany's power a little more than a year after Murphy's death, when he forced the nomination of James J. Walker for mayor in 1925 over the opposition of the venerable, white-mustached Brooklyn boss, John H. McCooey, who backed Mayor John R. Hylan for renomination in the city-wide primary.

In March, 1929, Olvany resigned the leadership. "Jimmy" Walker, facing a re-election campaign that year, selected Curry, a district leader, as Olvany's successor, and Tammany accepted the choice. Curry's five-year rule over Tammany covered the whole period of the damaging Seabury investigation of city affairs, from its first conception by Fiorello H. LaGuardia, during his unsuccessful campaign for mayor in 1929, to its culmination in Walker's resignation as mayor a year later.

Tammany's suicidal opposition to the national

Democratic administration in Washington, which was an important factor in LaGuardia's two subsequent re-elections in 1937 and 1941, and which also inspired the formation of the American Labor Party in 1936, began under Curry.

Tammany went to the 1932 Democratic National Convention in Chicago determined to bring about a second nomination of Al Smith for president if possible and, in any event, to stand to the last ditch against Governor Roosevelt. When Roosevelt won the nomination, Curry and his Tammany delegates left at once, without waiting for Roosevelt's arrival by plane to make his acceptance speech.

Nearly all of the big-city Democratic machines fought to prevent Roosevelt's nomination in 1932, but none of them was as bitter in its opposition, nor as sullen in defeat, as Tammany Hall.

The final major count against Curry's leadership was his insistence on renominating the blundering, comical Mayor John P. O'Brien (who had finished out Walker's term) to carry the Democratic banner against LaGuardia Fusionists in the 1933 election.

That stodgy, unimaginative nomination resulted in a wide-open split in the party throughout the city when the Roosevelt Democrats, led by National Chairman James A. Farley and Bronx Leader Edward J. Flynn, stepped in with an ill-advised effort to steal the election from what they thought were two unpopular candidates. The Farley-Flynn forces quickly organized the "Recovery Party" to back Joseph V. "Holy Joe" McKee, a nine-day wonder in New York city politics. But McKee went down faster than he had come up, and nothing has been heard of him in New York politics since that disastrous adventure. McKee took fully as many votes from LaGuardia as he did from O'Brien, who already was hopelessly beaten before McKee was thrown into the race.

On April 24, 1934, some eighteen months after Walker had resigned the mayoralty, one jump ahead of removal by Governor Roosevelt, Curry followed him into political oblivion. He was the first Tammany Leader ever to be voted out of that office by the normally docile and obedient members of the Executive Committee.

Curry sat in stunned silence listening to the roll-call, on which the district chiefs lined up 21 to 13 against him, with one man absent. No less than twenty-five of the thirty-five leaders had assured him within the previous twenty-four hours that he could count on them to the death.

The Seabury investigation, which turned up a wealth of stories of graft, sale of judicial nominations, etc. in Tammany and the city administration, did more harm to Curry's dignity than it did to his personal reputation. The high point of his

two-day ordeal on the witness stand was his ex-
cited charge of an attempted "crucification" of
the Democratic Party. About the only charge
against Curry which has been amply substantiated
is that he was not smart enough to cope with the
difficult political problems that arose during his
five-year Tammany reign.

A self-educated man who loved the power,
wealth and associations that went with the Tammany leadership, Curry suffered from an exaggerated conception of his own importance. In a
period that called for constructive, imaginative
leadership, Curry offered nothing but a stubborn
adherence to outworn ideas and personalities, and
an offended dignity whenever the voters refused
to accept his edicts. He remained active on the
fringe of Tammany politics, looking for revenge
and financing anti-organization district leadership
candidates, but with persistent lack of success.

At the time of Curry's expulsion, the two strongest district leaders, each ruling an entire section of
the city, were Edward J. Ahearn, leader of the
Fourth Assembly district and the dominant Tammany figure on the whole lower East Side, and
James J. Hines, boss of Harlem and of half a dozen
districts in addition to his own Eleventh. Both
were men of unusual personal ability. Their two
factions have continued to play a role in Tammany's internal politics right down to the present.

"Jimmy" Hines, a one-time blacksmith whose soft-voiced suavity betrayed nothing of his humble origin, was a personal friend of President Roosevelt and the political godfather of many men notable in New York affairs, including former New York Supreme Court Justice Samuel I. Rosenman, now a familiar White House adviser.

He was also, as District Attorney Dewey finally proved to the satisfaction of a New York jury, the political protector and financial beneficiary of a ring of gamblers who controlled the widespread "numbers" game in New York. Hines' conviction on that charge sent him to Sing Sing and gave Dewey his biggest single boost up the political ladder.

"Eddie" Ahearn, now dead, was the scion of one of Tammany's oldest families, always an element of strength in machine politics. The Ahearns were one of the last Irish families left in the Fourth Assembly district, which had become almost 100 per cent Jewish in population. Eddie was a clever leader. The Stand brothers, Bert and Murray, were his chief lieutenants. So great was Eddie's political potency that after his death in 1934 the Stand brothers were unwilling to let his name disappear from the district. They had his brother, Willie, who shared none of Eddie's political prowess or ability, installed as the district leader. Bert Stand became the real power in the district.

With the Tammany leadership left vacant after Curry's ouster, Eddie Ahearn became the strongest candidate for the post. National and State Chairman James A. Farley, patronage dispenser for the Roosevelt administration, turned thumbs down on him. Ahearn's associations on the East Side, an underworld stronghold, were such that Farley— and doubtless the President himself—considered him too vulnerable to assume the party leadership.

Hines did not aspire to the leadership, but put up one of his group, Washington Heights district leader John J. Kelly, whom President Roosevelt later appointed as United States Marshal in New York. Kelly proved unable to muster enough votes, and finally Hines and Farley united behind an independent district leader, James J. Dooling, who was then elected in a close count against Eddie Ahearn.

The Hines-Ahearn rivalry, which thus resulted temporarily in a victory for neither, was deep-seated. It arose out of many patronage disputes and conflicting ambitions, but in a sense it went all the way back to the idea, widely accepted in Tammany during Murphy's day, that there was a deep moral gulf between "honest graft" and "dirty money."

Honest graft, in Murphy's time, meant such pickings as cuts on public contracts, and "contributions" from candidates for public office. In a period of easier public morality, it came, by the early Thirties, to include payments for the "protection" of speakeasies and gambling. The political "take" from prostitution rings and extortion gangs remained definitely "dirty money." In 1934 the Hines faction in Tammany stood in the public mind for "honest graft." Some of Eddie Ahearn's less savory associates were shrewdly suspected of being tainted with "dirty money."

The Tammany-Roosevelt honeymoon which followed Dooling's election as leader was short-lived. It ended during the 1935 session of the New York State legislature, when the Democrats, for the first time in a generation, controlled not only the governorship but both houses of the legislature as well. (Al Smith once said it was unconstitutional for the Democrats to control the Assembly, a quip based on the under-representation of New York City in that body.)

State Democratic leaders were anxious to take advantage of the opportunity afforded by full party control at Albany to effect the long-delayed reapportionment of congressional and legislative seats, which had been overdue since 1920. But Tammany, which stood to lose several members of Congress and of the State Senate and Assembly, balked. Farley insisted that Dooling whip the organization and its Albany representatives into line. Dooling refused, and the Tammany-Roosevelt feud was on again. (After Thomas E. Dewey's election as governor in 1942 the legislature, controlled by Republicans, put through a reapportionment law, effective in the Fall of 1944, under which Tammany loses seven of its twenty-three assemblymen and three of its nine state senators.)

The next important shift in the Tammany balance of power came just before Dooling's death, and resulted from the maneuvering for the 1937 mayoralty campaign. Frank V. Kelly, leader of Brooklyn, Edward J. Flynn, of the Bronx, and Farley, in his capacity as state chairman, had agreed on the designation of Grover A. Whalen (who later retired in favor of Jeremiah T. Mahoney) as the organization candidate for mayor. Dooling had vainly urged the selection of Senator Royal S. Copeland, an anti-New Dealer, whose nomination would have been regarded as a direct slap by the New York City Democrats at President Roosevelt.

When the other county leaders insisted on supporting Whalen, Dooling, urged on by Al Smith, decided to enter Copeland in a city-wide primary contest against him. But in order to get the approval of the Tammany Executive Committee for his plan, which was opposed by Hines and his supporters, Dooling was forced to make peace with his old foes of what had been the Ahearn faction. That deal on the Copeland nomination marked an historic turning point in Tammany. What the lower East Side leaders got out of it was the final dominance of Tammany Hall, which "Eddie" Ahearn, himself, had never quite been able to attain.

Ahearn died a few months after Dooling's election in 1934, but his group still existed as the strongest single faction in Tammany Hall. Its dominant figure in 1937 was County Clerk Albert Marinelli, leader of the western half of the Second Assembly district in lower New York, a silent, grim ward politician of highly dubious connections.

Representative Christopher D. Sullivan, descendant of a once-powerful Tammany clan, was the leader of the eastern half of the Second Assembly district. But the Irish had long since moved out of the district and left it to the Italians and middle-European Slavs. "Christy" Sullivan remained as leader only by the favor of Marinelli, and only for such time as he might prove useful to Marinelli, who actually controlled the whole district.

Others in the Ahearn—now Marinelli—faction, included the leaders of four neighboring East Side districts, and of at least two uptown districts. Its principal figures, after Marinelli himself, were Bert Stand, former Alderman William "Billy" Solomon, who has since been convicted of bribery in a bi-partisan conspiracy to defraud the state through a monopoly on printing contracts, and Clarence Neal, leader of the Twentieth Assembly district and later the real power behind the Tammany throne and one of Aurelio's leading backers.

The deal between Dooling and the Marinelli faction was consummated at a meeting of the Tammany Executive Committee, when Dooling's decision to enter Senator Copeland in the mayoralty primary was ratified by a vote of 15 and 11/12 to 8 and 5/12.

Jimmy Hines, who had supported Dooling for leader, only to see him switch completely to the other side, came out of the meeting vowing to carry on the battle in the primary by supporting the Whalen city slate.

"I've been in primary fights before, and who knows more about a primary than Jimmy Hines?" he boasted to the waiting political reporters.

Marinelli, the new power in Tammany, was silent, but Clarence Neal answered Hines for him.

"That's all right with me," said Neal. "We'll abide by the primary, too, and we'll win."

Just how far Dooling had committed himself to Marinelli and Neal may never be known, for the Tammany leader, who had been ill for months, died within a week after that historic meeting.

In the midst of a city-wide primary fight, and with the Tammany Executive Committee itself split wide open, the Dooling leaders were forced to stick to their Marinelli alliance, or see Copeland's chances reduced to nothing.

And so, on August 2, 1937, after a series of futile maneuvers by Hines, the Executive Committee met and elected "Christy" Sullivan, Marinelli's man, as leader of the hall. The nomination was made by Clarence Neal and seconded by "Billy" Solomon.

County Clerk Marinelli had won his fight to control Tammany Hall, but his personal triumph was destined to be of brief duration.

Senator Copeland was defeated by "Judge" Mahoney, candidate of the Kelly-Flynn-Farley-Hines group, in the Democratic primary, and by Mayor LaGuardia in the Republican primary, where he had been entered by the anti-New Deal coalition, of which Al Smith was a leader.

In the general election campaign which followed, Thomas E. Dewey, Republican and American Labor Party candidate for the office of district attorney of New York County, attacked Marinelli with heavy broadsides. Dewey cited the undenied fact that scores of election captains and workers in Marinelli's Second Assembly district had criminal records. He branded Marinelli as "the political ally of thieves, pickpockets, thugs, dope-peddlers, and big-shot racketeers."

Dewey was elected as district attorney in November. Less than two months later Marinelli resigned his $15,000-a-year job as county clerk while Governor Herbert H. Lehman was considering the

petition of a citizens' committee for his removal.
Within a year he retired from his Tammany district leadership, also, and disappeared from public
life.

Clarence Neal, Marinelli's associate and ally,
stepped into the Italian's shoes as the dominant
member of the old East Side Ahearn faction, and
as the back-stage ruler of Tammany Hall. Bert
Stand, secretary of Tammany Hall, became his
right hand man, strategically situated inside the
county headquarters.

Neal is a smart, ruthless, two-fisted political
fighter who once drove a taxicab on the streets of
New York. After he went into politics he became
an inspector, and later, deputy commissioner in the
city department of markets. He has had no public
job for many years and the sources of his income
are obscure. Until the exposure of the $500,000
printing graft which led to the conviction of
"Billy" Solomon and a Republican deputy State
Controller in Albany, Neal had a modest income of
$5,000 to $6,000 a year as a salesman for the Burland Printing Company, which shared in the political monopoly of city and state printing contracts. The bribery scandal, never thoroughly
aired, put the Burland Company out of business,
but loss of his salesman's position apparently has
not embarrassed Neal. Nor have any of the official
investigations which have swept many of his col-

leagues into jail or political obscurity given Neal any real cause for concern. The printing investigation seemed threatening, but that bi-partisan scandal had so many ramifications that neither Governor Lehman, Mayor LaGuardia nor District Attorney Dewey cared to press the matter too closely.

During all of "Christy" Sullivan's rule in Tammany, lasting four and one-half years, Neal was clearly the boss. Sullivan obviously never felt free to make any important decision without consulting Neal. As a district leader, not a member of the ruling clique, once explained the situation to this writer:

"You go to Christy with a request. He listens to you and then says" (here the narrator imitated Christy's quiet, confidential manner and voice): " 'Let me think about that overnight. See me in a day or two.'

"That night," the district leader continued, "he'll talk to Clarence about it and when you go back to see Christy, he'll say" (again the super-confidential tone): " 'I'm sorry. I can't go along with you on that.' "

The fact that Sullivan lasted as leader for more than four years after Senator Copeland's defeat in the 1937 primary is a commentary on the power of even an unsuccessful and unpopular regime to maintain itself in office under the Tammany "boss" system. During the entire period, Sullivan never had the backing of a majority of the district leaders; but the opposition was always split into half a dozen factions, each unwilling to create a vacancy in the leadership to the possible advantage of one of the rival groups. Finally, in the Spring of 1942, after LaGuardia's third election as mayor and with a governorship campaign coming on, the district leaders met and voted Sullivan out of office, despite the fact that there had been no agreement on his successor.

A fairly complete "inside story" of how Representative Michael J. Kennedy won the leadership in the free-for-all scramble which followed can now be written, thanks to the evidence uncovered in the course of the scandal that followed the bipartisan nomination of City Magistrate Aurelio to a Supreme Court judgeship in the Fall of 1943.

At least half a dozen district leaders became serious candidates for the Tammany leadership as soon as Sullivan was kicked out. Neal, controlling the largest single bloc of votes, supported Representative James H. Fay, leader of one-third of the Twelfth Assembly district. Fay had a background of White House intimacy, having been the successful New Deal candidate against Representative John J. O'Connor, reactionary and obstructive chairman of the House Rules Committee, in President Roosevelt's famous "purge" campaign in the

1938 Democratic primaries. But the welcome sign at the White House had been pulled in, as far as Fay was concerned, about the time that he lined up with the Neal crowd in Tammany Hall.

President Roosevelt's choice for the vacant Tammany leadership, it soon became clear, was "Mike" Kennedy. As a member of the House of Representatives, "Mike" had voted consistently for the measures favored by President Roosevelt, even though his all-Irish district along Eighth and Ninth Avenues in mid-town Manhattan was far from being united in support of the President's pre-Pearl Harbor foreign policy. One of the younger and more progressive district leaders, Kennedy had argued for years that it was suicidal for Tammany to go on fighting the President. And he was regarded, on the basis of fervent "off the record" statements, as favoring a drastic clean-up of the bad spots in the Tammany organization.

The clearly indicated White House preference for Kennedy, backed by the implied promise (later handsomely made good) of Federal patronage for a "rejuvenated" Tammany, made Kennedy one of the two leading candidates for the leadership, Fay being the other. But with half a dozen other district leaders hoping to win the prize for themselves, neither Fay nor Kennedy was able to line up a majority of the total vote on the Executive Committee.

It was at this point, so far as the public record shows, that Frank Costello, a convict and big-time racketeer, became an important factor in the Tammany organization. Costello had been convicted in 1915 of illegally carrying a pistol and had spent ten months in jail. In the succeeding twenty-five years, during which he had only minor difficulties with the police, he had worked his way up through a career of gambling and large-scale bootlegging and slot machine operations, to membership in the select aristocracy of the underworld. The public had heard little of Costello, but his intimates had included such notorious public enemies as Al Capone, Arnold Rothstein, Joe Adonis, "Socks" Lanza, "Dutch" Schultz and Owney Madden.

Costello's illegal operations were highly profitable. In 1932 he paid New York State $305,000 in settlement of back income taxes and made a similar settlement, of an undisclosed but presumably much larger amount, of his previously unpaid Federal income taxes. Both settlements were made without embarrassing publicity for Costello and without any criminal prosecution for tax evasion.

From 1928 until early in 1934, Costello operated 500 or more highly profitable slot machines in New York City. Mayor LaGuardia, who took office in January, 1934, instigated a compaign to drive slot machines out of the city and personally attended to smashing several hundreds of them with sledge hammers and dumping them into New York harbor. But Costello merely moved his slot machine headquarters to New Orleans and continued operations from there, although he himself remained in New York City, where he had other highly questionable interests and many highly influential political friends.

Costello's principal Tammany "contact," as disclosed during the official and unofficial investigations of his part in bringing about Aurelio's nomination, was Clarence Neal. But at least three lesser district leaders, all from the lower East Side, were revealed as willing to accept "suggestions" from Costello in the conduct of their political affairs.

How Costello operated is revealed by an incident related by still another district leader whom the racketeer attempted, but failed, to bring under his influence. This leader is Assemblyman Patrick H. Sullivan, a young lawyer and protege of "Jimmy" Hines, now the leader in Hines' old district in Harlem.

Costello, of course, was exerting his influence in behalf of "Jim" Fay, Neal's candidate for the leadership. Late in February of 1942, Costello telephoned "Paddy" Sullivan and invited the district leader to his apartment on Central Park West. Sullivan, who had never met Costello, accepted the invitation. On his arrival he was at least mildly surprised when the door was opened by "Socks"

Lanza, a notorious fish market racketeer who had been active in lower East Side Tammany politics for years.

Costello came right to the point.

"I want to talk to you about a political matter," he said. "You know I'm very much interested in it."

"Paddy" Sullivan said he'd listen, whereupon Costello asked him whether he'd be interested in supporting Fay for the vacant Tammany Hall leadership. Sullivan replied that he was against Fay or anyone else who had Neal's support.

Costello then made this amazing and illuminating proposal: "Leave your vote with me and I'll deliver it the right way. If you do that, you'll never have to worry about a primary fight in your district. I'll give you all the manpower you need. You'll never have to worry about financing your leadership and your clubroom."

The offer was a tempting one. Even routine leadership fights in the primaries are expensive to repulse. Moreover, there was a clearly implied threat in Costello's offer. Sullivan realized that if he refused to "play ball" he probably would find a formidable and well-financed opposition candidate for his district leadership—as, in fact, he did in the next primary election.

Sullivan, nevertheless, promptly turned down the proposal. He had won the district leadership without outside help, he told Costello, and he would attempt to hold it the same way.

Unruffled, Costello closed the conversation by saying: "I'm sorry you can't play it my way. If you should happen to change your mind, call me up."

While efforts of this sort were being made—secretly, at the time, of course—on Fay's behalf, Kennedy was busy along somewhat different lines trying to win votes for his candidacy. One of the rival leadership aspirants was Representative Joseph A. Gavagan, a district leader. After a conversation with Mike, he got on the Kennedy bandwagon. He got his reward in 1943 when Tammany nominated him, and he was elected, as a Justice of the State Supreme Court, along with Aurelio.

These maneuvers failed to break the deadlock, however. What finally turned the trick was a quiet little meeting attended by Kennedy, Fay, Neal and Costello. Presumably they talked turkey. Shortly thereafter the Tammany Executive Committee was convoked, Fay withdrew in Kennedy's favor, and with Neal—and Costello—supplying the necessary votes, Kennedy was elected as leader.

With the Neal-Costello background of his election then entirely unknown to the public, Kennedy's election was widely accepted as the beginning of a new and better regime in Tammany Hall. President Roosevelt showed his favor by nominating James B. M. McNally, chairman of the Tammany Law Committee, to the office of the United States Attorney for the Southern District of New York, a job that Tammany had not held in years. The organization seemed well on its way toward re-establishing itself in public favor.

But to hundreds of Tammany insiders, it was clear that the big "reform" had been nothing but a shuffle of masks. The same crowd that had run the Hall when "Christy" Sullivan was leader was still running it with "Mike" Kennedy as leader. Clarence Neal was still the power behind the throne. Bert Stand, in his strategic spot as secretary of Tammany, was still Neal's agent at headquarters. And Kennedy, the would-be reformer, was as much a prisoner of the inner ring as Sullivan had been.

Then the lid blew off.

Late in August of 1943, District Attorney Frank J. Hogan, Tom Dewey's successor in that office, who had been investigating "Frankie" Costello's activities, made public the text of a tapped telephone conversation between Costello and Magistrate Aurelio.

Aurelio, just designated by Tammany and endorsed by the Republican organization for one of the vacancies on the Supreme Court bench, had called up Costello to thank him for his aid in landing the Tammany designation. And the Supreme Court judge-to-be had pledged "my undying loyalty" to the big-time slot machine racketeer and political fixer.

In the civic uproar that followed, an attempt was made to obtain Aurelio's disbarment in order to disqualify him for the bench in the event of his election. This was unsuccessful, but it did provide several days of sensational testimony in which Costello's influence in picking Tammany leaders as well as judicial candidates was spread on the public record.

Bert Stand, who had been one of the principal intermediaries in arranging the Aurelio nomination, resigned his job as secretary to the New York State Athletic Commission, but remained as secretary of Tammany Hall. Neal, another principal in the affair, simply shrugged the matter off and held on to his district leadership.

"Mike" Kennedy, in the opinion of many persons familiar with New York politics, had a unique opportunity really to clean up Tammany Hall by insisting on the resignations of Neal, Stand and the four or five other leaders subject to Costello's influence from the Tammany Executive Committee. But Kennedy, himself under obligation to Costello and the same group of leaders, failed to take advantage of the opportunity. Instead, Kennedy merely went through the motions of having the Executive Committee formally disavow Aurelio's candidacy and endorse the rival candidacy of Matthew M. Levy, the American Labor Party's candidate.

A measure of the sincerity of some of the Tammany district leaders in repudiating Aurelio was provided on election day, when Costello's friend was one of the seven successful Supreme Court candidates, out of a field of eleven.

Aurelio ran close to the top of the ticket in the Twentieth Assembly district, of which Neal is leader. He did equally well in the Fourth Assembly district, where Bert Stand is the real boss. He headed the list of non-sitting justices in the balloting in the First and Second Assembly districts. Dr. Paul F. Sarubbi, one of the leaders in the First district, and Jimmy Kelly, Greenwich Village night club proprietor and Marinelli's successor as leader of the Second Assembly district, were among the leaders who had been particularly intimate with Costello. All told, Aurelio got 103,600 votes on the Democratic line in Manhattan (the judicial district includes also the Bronx), while Levy polled only 21,119 votes on the special voting line set up for his Tammany supporters.

The election of Aurelio in the face of the civic indignation and the scandal caused by the Costello affair is partly explained by the popular, silent Tammany support among organization leaders and rank and file members. It was also due in some degree, however, to the feeling among New York's skeptical and worldly voters that too much of a political campaign had been made out of the case by the District Attorney who tried his case in the newspapers before he had even obtained an indictment.

Most of all, Aurelio's election was due, however, to the Republican Party's insistence on running its own candidate and thus splitting the opposition vote which might have elected Levy, the Labor Party candidate.

Tammany's future, however, is in doubt. As a result of a long line of scandals, topped by the Costello-Aurelio affair, the organization is at its lowest ebb in public esteem since the days of Tweed and Croker.

Nevertheless, Tammany continues to control the official Democratic party machinery in Manhattan. It can completely dominate the party primary and, therefore, control the party nominations for public office within its home county.

As long as Tammany remains under its present control, responsive to underworld pressure, if not complete dictation, Democratic candidates will suffer seriously in Manhattan on election day. What is more, Tammany is a definite liability to the Democratic party throughout New York State, and a potentially dangerous issue against the Democratic candidates in national elections.

President Roosevelt, party leaders in the rest of the state and many within Tammany itself, have expressed the desire to bring about a complete reorganization before the 1944 presidential campaign. But that is not easily accomplished. And a merely superficial clean-up, with the election of a new leader—Tammany's recently acquired method of seeking to win public favor—will no longer serve the purpose.

A move to expel Kennedy as leader got under way within Tammany immediately after the 1943 election. It was backed, however, by some of the same elements in the organization that had helped him get into the Aurelio nomination mess. Obviously, something more was needed than another "reorganization" arranged by Clarence Neal, with "Frankie" Costello in the background. But another "reorganization" arranged by Clarence Neal is precisely what happened with the election of Edward V. Loughlin as Tammany leader in January 1944. It was another personal victory for Neal, who acted as Loughlin's campaign manager, and for Bert Stand.

II

Brooklyn, the borough of homes and churches, always has suffered from a community inferiority complex because of its proximity to the wicked and glamorous borough of Manhattan. In politics, as in everything else, Brooklyn was content for years to take second place, with The Bronx, Queens and little Staten Island trailing along behind. But those days are gone, probably forever. In any gathering of New York State Democratic leaders today, the most important individuals are Frank V. Kelly, the tall, austere leader of Kings County (Brooklyn), and Edward J. Flynn, the courtly, smiling, but uncommunicative boss of The Bronx.

Kelly's power rises from the fact that he is the undisputed boss of the Democratic machine in the largest voting unit in New York State and in the country. Brooklyn has a population of 2,698,000, and in its best Democratic year, 1936, rolled up an astonishing election day majority of 509,000 votes for President Roosevelt over Alf M. Landon.

Flynn is equally dominant in the Democratic machine in Bronx County. From 1940 through most of 1942 his prestige as the spokesman for the Roosevelt administration in New York more than compensated for the fact that the Bronx ranks below both Brooklyn and Manhattan in population and voting strength.

But politicians, more than any other class of people, have to live in the present and not on the memory of past glories. Flynn's resignation as chairman of the Democratic National Committee, followed by the United States Senate row which blocked his appointment as Minister to Australia, effectively cut him down once more to the status of a county leader.

Frank Kelly's Brooklyn machine has survived the first decade of city rule by Mayor LaGuardia in far better shape than has Tammany Hall. One reason is that Kelly, while not sharing Flynn's un-wavering devotion to President Roosevelt, has avoided alienating masses of Brooklyn Democrats who follow and support the President's New Deal leadership. Another important factor is that the wells of patronage in Brooklyn, while they have fallen low, have never completely dried up.

The Brooklyn Democratic machine has managed to hold on to the Kings County District Attorney's office (important for more reasons than the patronage involved) despite determined efforts by LaGuardia to "give Brooklyn its own Tom Dewey." Except for a brief period, it also has controlled the Borough government with its very considerable number of small jobs. The current President of the Borough of Brooklyn, John Cashmore, is a district leader in the Kelly machine.

And, more important than either of these, from a patronage point of view, is the fact that Kelly has kept control over the elective judicial offices in Brooklyn, and, therefore, over many choice patronage plums, such as the appointment of secretaries to the justices and of a variety of court

clerks, not to mention the awarding of trustee-
ships and refereeships.

So far as personnel is concerned, the Kings
County court and the State Supreme Court within
Brooklyn come close to being Kelly's personal
property. In practice the Brooklyn county leader
has the absolute and final say in designating Democratic candidates for the bench to both these
courts. The candidates he selects must be nominated in the party primary and elected at the general election, but neither of these procedures is
much more than a formality under normal circumstances.

Brooklyn is entitled by precedent to seventeen
Supreme Court justices in the judicial district of
which it constitutes the major part, and there are
five judges of the Kings County Court. In each
court the terms are for fourteen years and the
judge's salary is $22,500 a year.

Kelly's recent choices for the Supreme Court,
all of whom are now wearing the judicial robes,
include Joseph Fennelly, who was a district leader,
Ivan Rubinstein, who served his apprenticeship as
chairman of the law committee of the Brooklyn
Democratic organization, Philip M. Kleinfeld and
Frank E. Johnson, both of whom earned Kelly's
favor by faithful work for the organization, Francis D. McGarey, another law committee chairman,
and Peter P. Smith, who seems to have been en-

titled to the job simply as a close friend of Kelly's. Another recently elected Supreme Court Justice, Nathan R. Sobel, was former Governor Lehman's counsel at Albany. He was named by Kelly at Lehman's personal request and in reciprocation for favors previously received by Kelly from the state executive.

Still sitting on the Supreme Court bench, in silent testimony to the thoroughness with which the "system" works, is John H. McCooey, Jr., son of Kelly's predecessor as county leader. The elder McCooey, fearing that people might think his son had been picked for the bench for some reason other than his outstanding ability, explained that the Brooklyn district leaders had unanimously urged the selection upon him. But just to make sure that the voters would have no chance to overrule the judgment of his district leaders, he went to the trouble of getting the Republican nomination for Junior, too. In return, the Democrats joined in a bi-partisan nomination of Meier Steinbrink, who at that time was the Republican leader of the county. The newspapers howled and the voters registered a mild protest, but both Steinbrink and young McCooey were, of course, elected.

The Kelly machine entered the 1944 campaign year in good condition. Of the twenty-four district leaders, nineteen held good public jobs, either elective or appointive. One of them, William J.

Heffernan, is a member of the bi-partisan New York City Board of Elections, which passes on the validity of primary designations and supervises the primary and general elections. Another, Henry Hesterberg, is a member of the New York City Board of Water Supply, also a bi-partisan agency. John Cashmore, as already noted, is the Borough President. Two are members of Congress—James Heffernan and Thomas H. Cullen, the latter a close friend of Mayor LaGuardia, who some years ago appointed Thomas H. Cullen, Jr., a City Magistrate. Two others—Irwin Steingut and Eugene Bannigan, are members of the State Assembly. Five district leaders are secretaries to Supreme Court justices. Four are clerks in the Brooklyn courts. Two are in the County Clerk's office, one as chief clerk and the other as deputy clerk.

In addition to the district leaders, an important functionary of the Kelly machine is John J. Lynch, who spends most of his time at Democratic County headquarters as aide and amanuensis to Kelly. Lynch is on the public payroll as secretary to Supreme Court Justice Philip Kleinfeld, who is more than happy to share his services with the boss.

Another important cog in the machine is Aaron L. Jacoby, to whom Kelly entrusts most of the details of organizing and running the election campaigns. Jacoby, a popular clubhouse orator as well as a good organizer, has held various county elective offices in Brooklyn and is now comfortable as chief clerk of the Surrogate's Court at $12,000 a year.

Kelly himself holds no public office. Machine politics being what it is, he doesn't need one. His chief source of income, so far as the record shows, is his $25,000 salary as resident vice-president of the Fidelity & Deposit Company of Maryland. This is a job which by tradition belongs to the Democratic leader of Brooklyn. The company does a general casualty and bonding business and, as might be guessed, does very well.

Kelly came from an humble family. His father was a horseshoer and Frank worked at the same trade for a while. Later he became a bank clerk. He worked his way up in the Brooklyn machine to the rank of district leader. After McCooey's death in 1934 he proved himself the strongest member of a triumvirate which conducted the county leadership for a brief period, and so inherited McCooey's mantle. He is a bachelor, a moderate drinker and likes an occasional trip to the races. He lives well, suffers from no lack of funds, but is not known as a heavy spender.

Kelly generally has given his political support to the programs and candidates favored by President Roosevelt. In the 1937 primary fight over the Democratic nomination for mayor, he joined Flynn and the leaders of Queens County and Richmond

(Staten Island) in backing Jeremiah T. Mahoney, who ran as a 100 per cent supporter of the President, against the late Senator Copeland, who was recognized as an anti-Roosevelt candidate. Mahoney won the nomination but lost the mayoralty election to LaGuardia. In 1940 Kelly supported the third term nomination of Roosevelt at the national convention in Chicago.

Kelly's major defection from the support of the President came at the Democratic state convention held at the St. George Hotel in Brooklyn in 1942, when the President sought the nomination of Senator James M. Mead to run against Dewey for governor while State Chairman Farley backed State Attorney General John J. Bennett for the nomination.

Kelly's support was the decisive factor in bringing about Farley's triumph and Bennett's nomination, but the incident apparently did not destroy friendly relations between the Brooklyn leader and the White House. The 100 per cent control over the big Brooklyn machine which Kelly demonstrated at the convention possibly dissuaded anyone from getting very angry with him.

Leaders of the Mead forces, with the open support of the President, were Governor Lehman, "Ed" Flynn and "Mike" Kennedy, whose election to the Tammany Hall leadership a few months earlier had been hailed as ending Tammany's long feud against the President. Backing Bennett were Farley and a small majority of the up-state county leaders, who had given Farley their pledge to support Bennett months before Mead entered the race. Mead's late entry into the race found Kelly, too, pledged to support Bennett, whose home is in Brooklyn.

There was little doubt that convention time found Kelly regretting his commitment to Bennett, and there was no doubt at all that a majority of the Brooklyn delegates to the convention would have preferred to vote for Mead. Some of the Brooklyn delegates, especially Assemblyman Irwin Steingut and "Nat" Sobel, counsel to Governor Lehman, had almost overwhelming personal obligations to follow Lehman's lead in supporting Mead.

Kelly, however, not only stood by his own pledge to Farley; he made it a test of personal loyalty to him for the Brooklyn delegates to stand fast for Bennett's nomination. And in an almost unprecedented demonstration of boss rule, he polled the votes of all but one of the Brooklyn delegates for Bennett. The lone exception was a close personal friend and one-time business associate of Senator Mead, who said that Kelly had sanctioned his vote for Mead on that personal basis.

Flynn, too, has come through the Democratic political depression of the LaGuardia era without disastrous weakening of the political machine he heads. He has kept his grip on the county prosecutor's office, the borough presidency and the courts, and so has had a minimum amount of patronage to hold the Bronx Democratic machine together.

The impression of Flynn as an uncouth ward politician, which became widespread during the Senate debate on his fitness to be Minister to Australia and Presidential ambassador in the whole Southwest Pacific area, was far from the truth. Flynn has his vulnerable points, but the uncouthness generally associated with ward politicians is not one of them. He is a cultured, well educated man of the world, quite at ease in any society. But so little was known about him, even after his two years in the spotlight as chairman of the Democratic National Committee, that his Senate critics, ably abetted by the opposition press, were able to spread a completely synthetic picture of him throughout the country.

The fault was principally Flynn's. For more than twenty years he had run the Bronx Democratic machine as his little private property for which he felt accountable to no one, including the public. Flynn was able to get away with this because the great metropolitan newspapers, published either in Manhattan or Brooklyn, had always found the affairs of Tammany Hall and the Brooklyn machine of much more interest than those of The Bronx. Until President Roosevelt persuaded him to become a "front man" in the third term campaign, Flynn took care to do nothing to attract attention. Both he as an individual and Bronx politics remained rather mysterious subjects even in his own city. He gave The Bronx reasonably good local government. His friends (and relatives) found comfortable spots on the payroll. His law firm did a phenomenal business. Nobody asked him embarrassing questions. Flynn found the situation perfect.

Once the President had forced Flynn into the national limelight as manager of the 1940 campaign, his political opponents naturally turned their guns against him. But they found very little at which to shoot. It was more than a year after the 1940 campaign that Flynn's foes made an incredible find. The "boss" had been doing a little fixing up around his country home at Lake Mahopac, north of the city, and the taxpayers, unwittingly, had footed the bill.

The great "paving block scandal" involved no great amount of public money, but it was the politician's dream of a perfect issue. The story of a political boss caught in the act of using city paving blocks, city trucks and city labor, to pave a "Belgian courtyard" at his country estate, was such a simple one that every truck driver, every laborer and every little home owner could comprehend it fully and immediately. The reaction of sophisticated politicans, on the other hand, was one of incredulity, followed by amazement that Flynn could have fallen for so ancient and obvious a piece of political stupidity.

There was no way for Flynn to get out of it. Everything he said simply made the matter look worse. When a Flynn district attorney presented the evidence to a Grand Jury consisting of Flynn subjects, which duly found that city property had been misappropriated but that no one—absolutely no one—was guilty of misappropriating it, the picture of the political boss caught with the goods and white washed by his loyal subordinates was complete.

The great "paving block scandal," skillfully used by partisan opponents, provided the clincher in preventing Senate confirmation of the diplomatic appointment which Flynn had earned by his devoted service to the President.

Flynn is a man of considerable wealth, most of it apparently derived from the law partnership of Flynn and Goldwater. Monroe Goldwater, his partner, runs the business which employs fifteen to twenty lawyers, and splits the profits with Flynn, who devotes little or no time to its routine affairs. Unquestionably the firm attracts much of its business because of Flynn's political prominence.

Monroe Goldwater also shares the perquisites of his partner's political leadership. He holds no po-

litical office, but his friends and relatives fare as
well in the matter of appointive public jobs as do
Flynn's. All in all, the Flynn and Goldwater association seems to be a happy one of mutual benefit.

III

The existence of New York's American Labor
party usually has been blamed, by those who disapproved of it, on James A. Farley. Actually, the
real father of the ALP was Mayor Fiorello H.
LaGuardia, the man who has most benefited from
it.

The Labor Party, destined to become an important element in state politics, was born at President
Roosevelt's campaign headquarters in New York's
Biltmore Hotel in 1936. Mayor LaGuardia, looking forward to his own re-election campaign as a
Republican-Fusionist a year later, felt some minor
embarrassment at the fact that his choice for
President was running as the candidate of the
Democratic Party. He conceived the idea of forming a new party as a medium through which the
liberal, anti-Tammany voters, and particularly the
members of organized labor, could support the
President without becoming contaminated by too
close association with the local Democratic machines.

No doubt the Little Flower, whose general political tendency is leftish, could see other, positive and permanent, reasons why it would be desirable to have a liberal third party operating in New York. But he didn't talk about that aspect of the matter.

"Jim" Farley, who could foresee future complications, strongly opposed LaGuardia's plan. He argued that organized labor was 100 per cent for Roosevelt anyway, and that it was unnecessary to do anything more than to form the usual labor committee as a branch of the Democratic campaign committee. The President, who shared LaGuardia's fondness for the new method, and who was perfectly willing to put a burr under the tail of the local Democratic organization, overruled Farley. And so the American Labor Party came into being.

The new party was founded on the nucleus of two of the oldest and strongest unions in New York—the International Ladies' Garment Workers Union, headed by David Dubinsky, and the Amalgamated Clothing Workers, of which Sidney Hillman is president.

Dubinsky and Hillman, dedicated to the same general political principles, but competitors in labor politics, have never openly headed the ALP; but they, with Mayor LaGuardia, have been the dominant influences behind the party scenes. As state chairman they installed Luigi Antonini, head of Local 89 of the I.L.G.W.U., which is composed entirely of garment workers of Italian birth or extraction. Antonini, a colorful character with a flowing black tie, never was more than a figurehead as state chairman. But he was a very good figurehead.

To do the actual work of putting together a party organization, the backstage managers selected Alex Rose, secretary of the United Hatters, Cap and Millinery Workers Union, affiliated with the American Federation of Labor (a happy fact during the days that the ALP was being called a purely CIO political organization). Rose demonstrated, in the next few years, not only that he was an organizer of extraordinary ability, but that he possessed political generalship considerably superior to that of the ordinary run of leaders produced by the major parties. He proceeded to build up a functioning organization of district leaders and clubs throughout New York City, where about 85 per cent of the state vote of the ALP is concentrated. The organization was set up along the same general lines as those of the major parties. Full use was made of union connections and loyalties in the designation of district leaders. In addition, the unions which enlisted in the party en bloc were formed into supplementary party machines, overriding district lines.

Although the ALP was conceived as a New Deal party, general manager Rose did not hesitate to take advantage of the temporary alliance with the Republicans in the LaGuardia re-election campaign of 1937.

He engineered deals on local candidates with the Republicans and Democrats alike, all of them to the net gain of the ALP. The party elected or shared in the election of five members of the State Assembly. In addition it came out of its first city campaign with the election of four of the twenty-six members of the New York City Council, chosen that year for the first time by proportional representation. And it provided 98,000 votes in New York County to help elect Thomas E. Dewey as district attorney.

In its first campaign the ALP had polled 274,924 votes for President Roosevelt, of which 238,845 came from New York City. In the 1937 municipal campaign, with anti-Tammany Democrats by the hundred thousand deserting their party to vote for Mayor LaGuardia, the vote on the ALP line soared to its high mark in the city, 482,790.

Governor Lehman was a candidate for re-election in 1938, with District Attorney Dewey as his opponent, and the ALP gave Lehman 419,979 votes. Since the governor won by only 65,000 votes, the importance of the Labor Party's contribution was self-evident. It was worth noting, too, that in New York County the ALP was able to do a complete turn-about from its support of Dewey for district attorney and to poll 73,000 votes against him as a candidate for governor.

In the third-term election of 1940, the balance-of-power votes again were cast on the ALP line. The party gave President Roosevelt 417,418 votes, while the President's total plurality over Wendell Willkie in the state was only 225,000.

Mayor LaGuardia was up for his third term in 1941, and the Labor Party came through with 435,374 votes to help keep him in City Hall.

In each of these elections the ALP ticket was headed by either President Roosevelt, Governor Lehman or Mayor LaGuardia, each of whom had a proven vote-getting ability in the Empire State, and each of whom was the candidate, at the same time, of one of the major parties. Even the leaders of the Labor Party were not sure how much of their strength depended on having a probable winner on the ticket, and how much of it was a genuine balance-of-power vote. In the 1942 state election they found out.

The Republicans again nominated their obvious candidate, Dewey, whom the laborites still refused to consider as being entitled to liberal support for governor. The Democrats rejected Senator Mead, President Roosevelt's candidate for the Democratic nomination, and put up Attorney General Bennett, to whom the ALP had also refused to give recognition as a liberal. So the Labor Party decided to put up a third candidate.

The nomination was tentatively offered to several potentially strong candidates—among them, Wendell Willkie—but all of them bowed out. Finally the laborites nominated Dean Alfange, a Greek-American lawyer. Alfange had been an unsuccessful Democratic-ALP candidate for Congress at a time when the country was stirred with admiration for the stubborn resistance the Greeks were putting up against Mussolini's invaders, but he was entirely unknown to the state as a whole. As a candidate for lieutenant governor the ALP nominated the Democratic incumbent, Charles Poletti, who was also the Democratic candidate for re-election.

When the election returns came in, ALP leaders were almost as much astounded as were the Republican and Democratic leaders. Alfange, who hadn't a ghost of a chance of election and who was not widely known, had received 409,047 votes on the ALP line. Poletti had received 418,764 votes and had come within 40,000 votes of being re-elected, despite Dewey's 630,000 plurality over Bennett.

On the surface, it seemed that the Labor Party had settled down to stay, and that its minimum of 400,000 votes would have to be taken into consideration in future Empire State elections. But, however it looked from the outside, the ALP still had difficult and perhaps impossible internal problems to solve.

During the "united front" period of Communist Party strategy, in 1936 and 1938, the New York State Communists had supported President Roosevelt and Governor Lehman so ardently that they lost their legal standing as a recognized political party. The election law defines a political party as one which polled at least 50,000 votes for its candidate for governor in the last preceding election. Having fallen below that number, the Communists were no longer entitled to a place on the ballot, although they could still nominate candidates by petition. And at the annual registration period there was no longer a "Communist Party" in which the party members could enroll.

In this situation, the Communists, while retaining their loyalty to their own unofficial organization, all enrolled as members of the ALP, and thereby obtained the legal right to vote in subsequent ALP primaries. There normally are close to 100,000 Communist voters in New York (actual party membership is secret, but undoubtedly is much smaller), and since the Communists are a highly disciplined and integrated body, this group became at once a dangerous threat to the program and integrity of the ALP.

Many of the garment workers, who formed the

bulk of the Labor Party's original membership, are former Socialists or Social Democrats. They had fought and beaten Communist efforts at infiltration in their union, and they were equally determined to fight any effort by the Communists to win control of the Labor Party.

The issue slumbered for a while during the "united front" period. But the isolationist, anti-Roosevelt stand which the Communists took during the early period of the European War brought it flaring into the open. The ALP was split right down the middle by the bitter ideological dispute between the isolationist "left wing" and the pro-Roosevelt "right wing."

The first attempt of the Communists to take over the machinery of the Labor Party failed largely because of the superior political generalship of Alex Rose, leading the fight for the Dubinsky-Hillman-Rose right wing. The primary battle in New York City was close and indecisive, but Rose was more skillful in electing favorable state committeemen in the up-state counties which contribute little to the ALP vote but which are legally entitled to representation in the state committee.

While the state organization was saved, a series of riotous party meetings and protracted court proceedings resulted in the leftists being recognized as the legal custodians of the party machinery in Manhattan. Representative Vito Marcantonio, who never has deviated from the Communist "line" in his votes in Congress, and Eugene Connally, an officer of the Communist-controlled National Maritime Union, were installed as leaders of the Manhattan organization. This was no ordinary factional struggle for control, but an ideological battle to the death. The rightists in the state committee, refusing to recognize the left wing Manhattan leaders as members of the ALP, but regarding them, instead, as piratical boarders, proceeded to set up their own parallel organization in New York County. The leftists could function within the county, but they were not recognized by the state organization. The left wing similarly formed county-wide district organizations to oppose the regulars in the Bronx and Brooklyn.

In the 1941 primary the decision was very close in Brooklyn, where the Labor Party polls its largest vote. Each faction claimed a majority of the 4,000 county committeemen who had been elected. When the committee met to organize, under arrangements made by the incumbent right wing officers, it was in a hall large enough to hold only about half of the committeemen who were eligible to attend and vote. Long before the hour set for the meeting the hall was filled to the doors with adherents of the right wing, who proceeded to reelect the incumbent county officers, while the leftists gathered helplessly outside the door.

After the 1943 primary, control of the committee was again in doubt. The left wing leaders appealed to the courts to order the meeting held in a hall large enough to accommodate all of the elected committeemen. But they had underrated the ingenuity of the right wing leaders, advised by the astute state secretary Rose. This time the rightists reversed the field and held the meeting in a hall large enough to hold not only the full county committee, but several thousand extra right wing adherents, who were on hand early. The right wing officials conducted the meeting to the full satisfaction of the galleries, and again were declared elected.

The leftists ran screaming to the courts and succeeded, eventually, in having the election voided. And in a subsequent meeting the left wing finally took over the Brooklyn organization.

The immediate future of the Labor party, and perhaps its eventual destiny, hinged in 1944 on the outcome of the state-wide fight for election of county committeemen in the Spring primary.

The prospects were that, if the left wing won control of the state committee, David Dubinsky and some 200,000 members of the Garment Workers' Union would pull out of the party, along with the able strategist, Alex Rose, and thousands of liberal, but anti-Communist members, represented by Professor George S. Counts, of Columbia University, who had succeeded Luigi Antonini as state chairman.

The picture was clouded by a rapidly developing split between Hillman and Dubinsky. Hillman, as chairman of the nation-wide political action committee of the CIO, had proposed that the basic structure of the American Labor Party be altered by admitting all CIO unions to party affiliation, and placing control of the party in a trade union committee. Hillman's plan was enthusiastically seconded by the left wing leaders, but it was opposed by Dubinsky, Rose and Professor Counts on the ground that it would immediately admit leaders of Communist-dominated unions to posts of party responsibility and leadership.

Mayor LaGuardia, who has divided his support impartially between the left and right-wing factions, seemed likely to prove the key figure in whatever temporary expedient—or permanent solution—might be worked out in the effort to retain the Labor Party as an effective New Deal instrument in New York politics.

2

BOSS PLATT'S SHOES

For thirty years there has been a strong element of envy in the righteous cries New York State Republicans have emitted against boss rule in the Empire State.

The Grand Old Party had once known the combination itself, but it was lost with the death of Thomas C. Platt in 1910. Boss Platt was a man of heroic mold, a contemporary and peer of Pennsylvania's Boies Penrose. He left no heir. For a generation after his death the GOP state machine, which had completely dominated the Empire State at the turn of the century, steadily deteriorated. It was not until 1935 that a worthy successor to Platt stuck his head above the level of the little leaders who had been attempting to run the Republican organization.

Edwin F. Jaeckle, who became chairman of the

Erie County (Buffalo) Republican organization in that year, has increased his sphere of influence steadily since then. The vote machine which he gradually built up, and which he dominates, has been an important factor in the parallel decline of Democratic power, and in the final overthrow of the Smith-Roosevelt-Lehman regime at Albany.

The Republican state organization has always consisted of a group of more or less strong machines in the upstate cities of Buffalo, Rochester and Syracuse, and of rural county organizations which were virtually unopposed and which drew their strength from the fact that New York farmers vote Republican as habitually as Southerners vote Democratic.

In New York City, Republican strength has been concentrated in the two Assembly districts embracing the wealthy residential areas along Park Avenue and north of Washington Square. The county organizations within the city usually have been controlled by the rival Democratic machines.

John J. Knewitz, Republican leader of The Bronx for a generation, held a $9,000-a-year job as Commissioner of Records, a job that was completely at the disposal of Boss Flynn's Democratic organization. In return, the Knewitz Republicans made no trouble for Flynn.

Samuel S. Koenig, veteran and cooperative Republican leader of Manhattan, profited through

legal work and receiverships thrown his way by
Charles F. Murphy and subsequent Tammany leaders. His brother, the late Morris Koenig, was placed
on the General Sessions (County court) bench at
$22,500 a year by a bi-partisan endorsement. His
son, Ira Koenig, became clerk to Supreme Court
Justice Samuel Hofstadter, whom "Sam" Koenig
and Tammany Leader Curry combined to put on
the bench in one of the famous bi-partisan deals of
New York's history. The "Hofstadter-Steuer deal"
provided a classic example of Republican-Tam-
many cooperation.

Hofstadter, Republican state senator from the
"silk stocking" Park Avenue district, was chairman
of the legislative committee which investigated the
city's affairs in 1930-32 with Samuel Seabury as
committee counsel. Curry, in one of the overly
clever maneuvers which hastened his downfall, decided to take investigator Hofstadter out of the
1932 city campaign by nominating him for the
bench, and Koenig readily assented. As the apparent quid pro quo, Koenig delivered the Republican
nomination for a second Supreme Court vacancy
to Aaron Steuer, son of Tammany's legal adviser,
Max D. Steuer. Both were elected, but the deal so
outraged independent voters that its net effect was
to further discredit both Curry and Koenig.

Following Boss Platt's death, the Bull Moose
split in 1912 and the development of prohibition as

a major issue helped to upset the old Republican balance of power between up-state and New York City. The emergence of Alfred E. Smith as the most popular figure of his day started the Democrats on their twenty years of unbroken success in state elections.

During the twenties and thirties, the old GOP machine declined because of lack of patronage and because of the espousal by its leaders of the unpopular side of such issues as the development of the state's water power resources and the social welfare program advanced by the Democrats.

James A. Farley, as state chairman during the Roosevelt regime at Albany after 1928, further strengthened the Democratic position—and weakened the Republican grip up-state—by building at least the skeleton of a Democratic organization in every one of the rural counties. Yet, so firmly imbedded was the Republican tradition in rural New York that in 1936, when President Roosevelt carried everything except Maine and Vermont, and swept the Empire State by a 1,114,000 plurality, he carried only eight of the fifty-eight couties outside New York City. And those eight were in the big urban centers upstate.

The basis of Republican strength still existed in New York. What was lacking was organization and leadership.

Before Jaeckle's emergence as state leader in

1938, the Republican State Committee had had six chairmen in ten years. The kaleidoscopic succession of leaders ranged from H. Edmund Machold, utility magnate and one of the continuing powers in the Republican organization, who came out of his political back room to lead the fight against "Al" Smith for President and Franklin D. Roosevelt for governor, to W. Kingsland Macy, open foe of the public utility wing of the party. Macy was put in as state chairman in an effort to remove the power trust stigma from the party, and then thrown out of the job when the utility companies found that he was serious about the matter. Apart from Machold there was not a strong man in the batch of leaders. The names of William J. Maier, Melvin C. Eaton and William S. Murray, all of them state chairmen during the thirties, are virtually forgotten.

"Ed" Jaeckle is a state leader of entirely different mold.

His political career began in 1917, when, at the age of twenty-three, he was elected to the Erie County board of supervisors. Three years later he resigned as supervisor to become clerk of the board, a position which gave him more opportunity to build up a personal following among the ward leaders. In 1926 he became a member of the state committee and felt himself strong enough to strike out for himself. He managed the campaign of an anti-organization candidate for county treasurer, one Charles Ulrich.

It was this step which led him toward financial independence and the pleasant sense of security that is so useful to anyone with a preference for aggression rather than appeasement. Ulrich, elected treasurer, appointed Jaeckle to the county post of collector of back taxes, a fee-paying job no more strenuous than clipping coupons.

From 1928 through 1933, when the legislature abolished the job, Jaeckle salted away $154,506 in fees. At the same time he developed a flourishing law practice on the side. His present income from his law practice and investments can only be guessed at.

The Erie County Republican machine had been falling to pieces under county chairman Fred A. Bradley, who also was customs collector at Buffalo during the period when the city was the center of rum-smuggling from Canada. The amiable, pipe-smoking William J. Hickey, who succeeded Bradley in 1932, did nothing to repair the party organization.

The upward climb of the party in Erie County, and in the state, can be traced from September 24, 1935, when a small group of moneyed Republicans engineered a coup which put the aggressive and moneyed Jaeckle in as county chairman in place of the easy-going, philosophical Hickey. The latter was consoled by being nominated, and duly elected, as a Justice of the Supreme Court.

Jaeckle began to whip the party organization back into shape. His hard-hitting methods put the Buffalo machine workers on notice that they were expected to deliver. And Jaeckle, a calculating man who overlooks no angle of race, religion and geography, gave them the sort of leadership that helped them produce. At the 1936 national convention, Jaeckle promoted himself to state-wide prominence by firing a carefully timed broadside against Charles D. Hilles, New York's superannuated member of the Republican National Committee and a faithful devotee of Hooverism in the party. Jaeckle called Hilles a tool of Wall Street, a catspaw for the corporations, and whatever else he could think of at the moment. He demanded that Hilles be removed immediately.

Two years later Jaeckle had acquired sufficient stature to be made chairman of the executive committee of the state committee, a post newly created for him and one which made him state leader in fact, but not in name. Jaeckle promptly set up headquarters in the Ten Eyck Hotel at Albany, where he spent two days a week while the state legislature was in session. For the first time in three decades, a state boss frankly ran the legislature, shaping the GOP program, and seeing that it was executed. The Albany Legislative Correspondents'

Association included in its annual satirical show a song with the refrain: "You've gotta get Jaeckle's O.K."

Meanwhile, things were happening in the Republican organization in New York City.

Kenneth F. Simpson, leader of the "silk stocking" Fifteenth Assembly district, but a practical politician who could make himself understood on Tenth as well as on Park Avenue, had led a revolt against the Republican practice of playing "minority politics" in New York County. In a primary fight in 1935, Simpson ousted "Sam" Koenig as New York County chairman, and took over the job of building a genuine Republican Party in the city.

Almost single-handed, Simpson kept the city GOP from the suicidal course of throwing Mayor LaGuardia overboard in 1937 and nominating a "regular Republican" candidate for mayor. The Republican "clubhouse loafers," as LaGuardia publicly called them, had ample grievance against the Mayor. But, as LaGuardia well knew, they were too weak to be able to retaliate for his jibes and abuses.

Simpson bludgeoned and reasoned the district leaders into line, promoted "Tom" Dewey's nomination for district attorney and squeezed two "regular Republicans" from his own district—Newbold Morris and Stanley M. Isaacs—onto the LaGuardia ticket as candidates for the offices of president of the city council and Manhattan borough president, respectively.

Simpson also scandalized the Hoover Republicans by making deals on district candidates across the board with the American Labor Party, which was also supporting LaGuardia. And for the first time, thanks to Simpson's efforts, a Fusion victory in New York City was turned, to a considerable extent, into a Republican victory as well. Moreover, the groundwork was laid at last for the formation of a Republican organization in the city that would be at least partially independent of the Democratic machines.

Dewey and Jaeckle were brought together in the 1938 campaign, and each recognized the worth of the other. Dewey saw in Jaeckle the astute, realistic and forceful politician he needed to service the state machine which both were building, and Jaeckle recognized in Dewey the popular figure he required in order to enlarge the scope of his own political power. Both of them had plenty of resilience to withstand the blow of Dewey's defeat for governor in 1938, and to go on building for the next campaign.

J. Russell Sprague, leader of Nassau County on Long Island, was brought into the line-up as the third member of what has come to be known as the Jaeckle-Sprague-Dewey state machine. Nassau

County is the wealthiest community in the country, and the richest source of Republican campaign contributions. Sprague is in complete control of the party's machinery in the county, and he knows from long experience how to tap its sources of party wealth to the best advantage.

Just as everything seemed to be ticking along smoothly, a bitter personal row broke into the open between Dewey and Simpson, who by then had succeeded Hilles as New York's member of the National Committee.

Dewey thought that Simpson was taking entirely too much credit for his election as district attorney, and he went to some pains to let Simpson know that, so far as he was concerned, Simpson was a pretty insignificant political leader. He made it plain that Simpson could look elsewhere for patronage favors. Simpson concluded that Dewey was a conceited young whippersnapper with too big ideas, who would have to be put into his proper place.

The feud developed into a state of implacable hostility on both sides. Simpson's wife was credited with a bon mot that was repeated all over the country: "You have to know Dewey well in order to dislike him."

As the 1940 national convention approached, Simpson threw everything he had into an enthusiastic campaign to puncture Dewey's presidential boom. After arranging to split the New York delegation away from Dewey as far as possible, he took to the road, and tirelessly sowed suspicion of New York's "favorite son" among party leaders from other states. The success of Simpson's strategy, including the split delegation from his home state, was largely responsible for the poor showing Dewey made at the Philadelphia convention.

Just before the convention, Dewey and Jaeckle hit back. They called the state delegation together, summarily ousted Simpson as National Committeeman, and installed Sprague in his place.

It was some months later that Herbert Hoover, now a resident of New York's Waldorf Astoria Hotel, decided to do his bit for Republican amity in the state. Apparently deluded into believing that everything would be fine if Dewey and Simpson could be induced to kiss and make up, Hoover first approached Dewey with that in mind.

"It is a time to be broad, to think of the larger goal of party welfare," said Hoover, in substance. "Simpson means well, and I understand is eager to be friends with you again, so why not stop acting like little boys and do the big thing?

"I know that Kenneth has referred to you in disparaging terms in that article in *Life* magazine," Hoover went on, "but he was a little overwrought."

"Yes," said Dewey, "and have you read the interview *PM* had with Simpson in the Sunday issue?"

"No," said Hoover.

"Well, in it Simpson said that the party has some excess baggage named Hoover which must be overthrown if the party is to survive."

The ex-president reddened, sputtered, and gave up his self-appointed role as peace-maker.

After the 1938 defeat and the set-back at Philadelphia, Jaeckle went on methodically building up the Republican machine throughout the state, and tightening his grip on its controls. The Buffalo machine was oiled to such perfection that the Republicans now have fourteen of the fifteen common council seats and a clear control in twenty-one of Buffalo's twenty-seven wards.

Jaeckle spends half of each week at home and during the rest of the time shuttles back and forth to New York City, to Albany when the legislature is in session, and to other parts of the state. He is in frequent touch with all of the county chairmen, and succeeds in giving them the double impression that he is devoted to their individual interests, and that he is quite capable of breaking any one of them, politically, who might attempt to put anything over on him.

Only one of the county leaders has, in fact, consistently held himself free from the Jaeckle machine. He is Rolland B. Marvin, leader of Onondaga County and former mayor of Syracuse. Marvin joined Simpson, in 1940, in backing Wendell Willkie for the nomination for President. During 1943, the Dewey-Jaeckle combine tried to clear up this area of disaffection by starting a backfire against Marvin in his home county. They met with only indifferent success.

Simpson, the biggest hurdle in the Dewey-Jaeckle path, was unexpectedly removed by death in 1941, just after he had taken his seat in the House of Representatives as successor to Bruce Barton. In Simpson's place as New York county leader the machine installed Thomas J. Curran, whom Dewey later appointed as Secretary of New York State.

In Brooklyn the machine has an equally compliant leader in John R. Crews, a former middleweight prizefighter who has taken into politics all of his skill at ducking and weaving. "Johnny" Crews concerns himself little with statesmanship, but he is always alert to take tactical advantage of any opportunity to improve his political fortunes. Thus, he used his support of Mayor LaGuardia in the 1937 mayoralty primary to get himself appointed to the bi-partisan New York City Board of Elections, an $8,000-a-year post and one carrying both political prestige and power.

"Johnny's" greatest concern, however, is to insure the continued re-election of his twin brother,

Robert J., to the State Assembly. Brother "Bobby" runs in a normally Democratic district, and the election figures support a suspicion that his regular re-elections have been at the expense of other Republican candidates in whom the county leader has had a less personal interest.

Dewey's election as Governor in 1942 provided the first fruits of victory for the new state machine. Backed up by Jaeckle, Dewey adopted the policy of giving the top state jobs to able men—going outside of politics to find some of them. But the secondary jobs, the real life-blood of a political machine, have uniformly been parceled out through the organization.

The most significant of all Dewey's appointments was that of Miss Louise G. Gerry, vice chairman of Jaeckle's Erie County organization, as one of the three members of the state civil service commission, which supervises a vast field of local, as well as state, patronage.

As chairman of the commission, Dewey appointed J. Edward Conway, former assemblyman and political lieutenant of the late Philip Eltinge, a colorful leader of the GOP Old Guard in the state.

The special election of a Lieutenant Governor in 1943, a political off-year, made necessary by the death of the incumbent, provided the final proof that New York, after thirty years, again had a powerful and smoothly functioning Republican state machine.

Governor Dewey, who likes to explore the ground ahead thoroughly and cautiously before taking a forward step (he has never run for office without employing the private services of the Gallup poll to assay his chances of election), tried to avoid the special 1943 election. He interpreted the state constitution as permitting the majority leader of the state senate to fill out the term of the Lieutenant Governor. But the State Court of Appeals, still manned by a majority of Democrats, overruled him.

On election day, Dewey was in a state of near-collapse. He confided in members of his staff that he would be happy with a 5,000 plurality for the Republican candidate, preacher-Senator Joe R. Hanley.

Dewey didn't know how well Jaeckle had builded. Hanley's victory margin was a whopping 341,372.

The New York City voting had gone about as anticipated, with the Democratic machines turning in a meager 320,327 plurality for the Democratic-ALP candidate (898,360 to 578,033).

What upset all calculations was the tremendous turn-out in the Republican areas outside New York City, and the overwhelming majorities for the Republican candidate. Erie County turned in a

Republican plurality of 59,000. Sprague's Nassau County voted 98,000 to 26,000. Wealthy, suburban Westchester went for Hanley 115,000 to 52,000. The Suffolk vote was 42,000 to 15,000. In some of the smaller, and entirely rural, counties the Jaeckle machine turned in majorities as high as five to one. All told, the vote outside New York City was 1,246,869 to 585,170, a better than two-to-one vote, and an up-state majority of 661,699 to stack up against the city's skimpy 320,327 for the Democrats.

By ten o'clock on election night Dewey was able to sit up and take nourishment. By midnight he was giving some private but serious reconsideration to the prospects for 1944.

3

THE O'CONNELL RING

THE 1944 presedential election year opened with sensational political events brewing in New York.

Governor Dewey, who had scampered far up the ladder as a youthful crusader against "criminal political organizations," was on the warpath again. Along with his residence, the governor had moved the scene of his crusade for civic virtue to the state capital at Albany. The immediate objective of his 1944 campaign was the complete destruction of the O'Connell machine which for more than twenty years had preserved Albany and Albany County as a citadel of Democratic strength in the Republican territory of upstate New York.

The Albany Democratic organization obviously was ripe for the killing. No one in or out of the machine had any doubt that the many-pronged investigation being pressed by Dewey would result in the disclosure of a political mess. The only question was whether the cornered Democratic bosses would have the determination and the ability to fight back and to embarrass Governor Dewey by the exposure of an almost equally unsavory condition in Dewey's own party.

During most of the twenty years that the Democrats had run the municipal and county governments at the capital, the Republicans had controlled one or both of the houses of the state legislature. If there was corruption in the municipal government, there was corruption in the state legislature, too, and the Democrats seemingly were in a strategic position to retaliate. The Democrats, still in control of the county law enforcement machinery, seemingly were in a strategic position to retaliate for Dewey's campaign of exposure against them.

Both exposure and counter-exposure had been threatened for years, but nothing ever had come of it beyond the usual campaign charges, supplemented by a growing collection of whispered rumors. Now it appeared at least likely that some of the long-promised sensations would be at last unveiled.

Four brothers, Edward J., Daniel P., Patrick J. and John J. O'Connell founded the Democratic machine at a time when a strong Albany Republican organization bossed by William Barnes was begining to break up under the double impact of graft charges and inner rivalries. "Dan" O'Connell, last of the brothers to exercise political power in Albany, was the first of them to break through the lines of the dying Republican machine. Just back from World War service in the Navy, he campaigned in his sailor's uniform in 1919 and won election as one of the three members of the city's tax assessment board. The post was a significant one in view of the use which the O'Connells later made of the tax assessment rolls as a means of subduing Albany and making its citizens toe the mark.

The O'Connells completed their conquest of the city with the election of a Democratic mayor, William Hackett, in 1921. Throughout the state Democratic regimes of Governors Alfred E. Smith, Franklin D. Roosevelt and Herbert H. Lehman the brothers not only controlled their own political domain but were admitted to full partnership with the New York City bosses in the state-wide decisions of the party.

While "Ed," "Dan" and Patrick devoted their attention to the political machine, the fourth brother, John "Solly" O'Connell, went in for big-time gambling.

Fraudulent voting by means of heavily padded registration lists and ballot-box stuffing is one of the methods by which the O'Connell machine has maintained its grip on the city and on Albany

County. For many years the number of persons registered and the number of votes cast in Albany in proportion to population has been the highest in the country. The explanation does not lie entirely in political awareness and civic mindedness on the part of Albany's residents. The population of the city of Albany in 1940 was 130,577 and 79,821 votes were counted, an incredible figure amounting to more than 61 per cent of the entire population. The theoretical maximum would be about 66 per cent—if every resident over twenty-one years of age voted.

An even more powerful weapon in the machine's continued control of the city has been the use of tax assessments to reward property owners who voted right and to punish those who registered as Republicans. Wise and frugal home owners in New York's capital city long ago learned not to enroll as Republicans. In 1938 only 6,930 of the city's registrants admitted their Republicanism, as compared with 51,035 enrolled Democrats. Presumably, few of the 6,930 Republicans were property owners. It was too costly.

Preliminary investigation of the assessment rolls in 1943, after racket-buster Dewey took office as the first Republican governor since 1922, not only revealed hundreds of cases of gross discrimination, it also disclosed the pattern by which the O'Connell organization operated the racket. Hundreds of protests or appeals for reduction of assessments were discovered to have been notarized by Democratic ward leaders or county committeemen or by office holders or favored lawyers of the O'Connell machine. The appellants thus identified as friends of the organization received uniformly favorable consideration. Large taxpayers usually hired O'Connell lawyers to represent them in assessment appeals.

Regularly each year, from 1932 to 1943, the New York Central Railroad received a reduction of $1,000,000 in its Albany assessment. Each year the higher figure was fixed. Each year the railroad appealed. Each year it was represented by Robert E. Whalen, an attorney who is one of "Dan" O'Connell's closest advisers. And each year it received the usual reduction.

At one point during this same period, the city was faced with a court action in which another taxpayer sought to have the rule established that assessment valuations, once duly fixed, could not be raised except on the ground of some definite increase in the value of the property. This was an effort to break up the practice of annual increases in assessments and annual reductions on appeal. The lawyer whom the city hired as a special counsel to oppose this action was the same Robert E. Whalen.

In October, 1942, Dewey, running for governor, devoted a campaign speech to the Albany assessment racket and promised to clean it up if he were elected. Richard J. Lewis, who had been tax assessor since 1923, listened to the speech on the radio. He suffered a stroke later that night and died within two weeks.

During the 'twenties the O'Connell brothers operated the highly profitable "Albany baseball pool," a numbers lottery which finally was broken up by Federal prosecution after it had grown beyond state lines and spread over the whole Middle Atlantic and New England states. "Dan" O'Connell served thirty days for contempt of court after refusing to answer questions in the course of the Federal prosecution.

The O'Connell's biggest bath of national publicity—prior to 1944—followed the kidnapping of John J. O'Connell, Jr., the son and namesake of "Solly," in 1933. Junior, then twenty years old, was taken to Hoboken and held until his family raised $40,000 to ransom him. One version of the story was that "Solly" had welshed on a bet and that Junior was "snatched" as a method of inducing prompt payment.

During the time that Junior was being held, the kidnappers, by note, requested his family to publish a list of well known racketeers from which they could select an intermediary to carry on ransom negotiations. The first two lists were rejected, so that the O'Connells finally published thirty names before a satisfactory intermediary was chosen. Several of those listed were members of the O'Connell organization and one of them, James J. "Bindy" Reilly, leader of the Eleventh Ward, later on was appointed clerk of the New York Senate.

Throughout their political career the O'Connells have had a prosperous business in the Hedrick Brewery, which is owned in the family, and managed, at present, by John J. O'Connel, Jr. The Hedrick company has enjoyed a complete monopoly on the sale of draft beer in Albany.

The machine has an equally thorough monopoly on Albany jobs. There are nineteen wards in the city—and there are nineteen Democratic aldermen. The Board of Aldermen is one of the most harmonious legislative bodies in the country. No one can remember when the last dissenting vote was cast. O'Connell henchmen hold all other city jobs, as well, and Democrats occupy 32 of the 39 seats on the Albany County board of supervisors.

The Albany machine, presenting on a relatively small canvas virtually all of the evils of boss rule as they have been known in the metropolitan centers of New York, Chicago and Philadelphia, has been a constant target of Republican campaigners since the 'twenties.

The unbelievable registration totals, the tax extortion and favoritism, the O'Connell beer monopoly, the admitted gambling records of the brothers, the convictions obtained in the baseball pool case and the unsavory connections exposed by the kidnapping of "Solly's" son, have been hammered home time and time again during state as well as local campaigns.

But the machine's grip never has been weakened. It has continued to turn in Democratic pluralities of 20,000 to 40,000, and its bosses have been among the recognized rulers of the Empire State during the long Democratic regime.

"Ed" O'Connell, who shared power equally with "Dan" for many years, died in 1939. He was succeeded as county chairman by young John, the kidnap victim of six years earlier. But John concededly is a mere dummy for "Uncle Dan," the real boss of the machine. "Dan" perhaps chose to decline the official position of leader because of the annoying habit of Republican campaigners of referring to him as "the twice convicted Dan O'Connell"—both references being to contempt convictions in connection with the Federal baseball pool prosecution.

But "Dan" continued to exercise openly his power as the actual leader of the upstate Democratic stronghold. After Governor Lehman had flatly refused to run for re-election in 1938, "Dan" was present with State Chairman James A. Farley and the New York City Democratic leaders when the big bosses of the state gathered in Lehman's room at the convention hotel in Rochester and prevailed upon him to accept the nomination.

During the ensuing campaign, Republican candidate Dewey described in flavorsome detail how the "twice convicted" Albany leader sat on Governor Lehman's bed and pleaded with him to run just once more. "Jim" Farley disputed the accuracy of this description. "Dan," he said, "didn't sit on the bed—he sat on a chair." Dewey cheerfully accepted the correction.

Albany turned in a Democratic plurality of 28,000 in the 1938 election, accounting for almost one-half of Governor Lehman's slim margin of victory. Four years later Dewey was elected as Lehman's successor and he promptly began to translate into action his promises to clean up Albany County. But whether from necessity or design, Dewey delayed the real investigation until the Spring of 1944.

During the Fall of 1943 he began to prepare for the showdown through the medium of three preliminary investigations. A special election frauds bureau of the attorney general's office seized the Albany registration books for 1942; the state tax department opened a formal inquiry into assessment abuses, and the state controller began hearings on a charge that municipal officials had diverted capital expense funds illegally to meet current expenses.

Democratic District Attorney Delaney countered by impanelling a grand jury to probe into the touchy subject of expenditures by the legislature, and particularly by legislative committees, which usually have been controlled by Republicans.

The make-up of the grand jury emphasized the complete O'Connell dominance over everything in Albany County. Of its twenty-one members, three were contractors who do business with the municipal government and twelve were Democratic ward leaders, committeemen or party workers. Among the twelve were four who held city jobs and four who had been discharged from state jobs—and replaced by Republicans—after the Dewey administration took over the state government.

Governor Dewey met the challenge of the Delaney grand jury investigation by taking the whole matter out of the hands of the Democratic district attorney and appointing a Republican lawyer, Hiram C. Todd, as special prosecutor to carry on the investigation of legislative spending.

In the 1943 election Dewey stationed one hundred state troopers at the registration booths and later at the polling places on election day.

The governor assured Albany residents that for

the first time they would be able to vote without
fear of intimidation or reprisals from the Democratic machine. Whether Albany didn't quite believe him, or whether it really likes the O'Connell
rule would be hard to say. Anyway, the voters
turned in the usual 21,000 to 25,000 majorities for
the O'Connell candidates for city and county offices.

And the process of investigation, under the
threat of counter-investigation, speeded up as the
calender turned into the presidential election year.

4

HAGUE'S HUNDRED THOUSAND

WHEN CHARLES EDISON wound up his three-year term as Governor of New Jersey on January 18, 1944, the principal item of unfinished business which he bequeathed to his successor was a well developed, but still uncompleted campaign to rid the state of the Frank Hague dictatorship.

Governor Walter E. Edge, the 73-year-old Republican who took over the executive offices, was pledged both by his campaign promises and his party platform to carry on the fight that had been started by Edison, the Democrat.

Hagueism, as Edison could testify, offered stout defenses against anyone who might try to liquidate it. In its quarter-century of growth, it had become more than a nearly perfect political machine. On its home grounds in Jersey City and Hudson County it encompassed education, religion, commerce and the arts. It had become a way of life—

more than slightly tinged with fascist-like dictator-ship—in what has been called America's most ex-pensively governed and worse run city.

Mayor Frank "I-am-the-law" Hague, its boss and fuehrer, showed only slight external signs of damage as a result of the three years of open war-fare waged against him by Governor Edison. Se-curely entrenched behind his 100,000-vote machine plurality in Hudson County, in firm control of the state Democratic organization, buttressed by a working alliance with President Roosevelt, Hague settled down to outlast Republican foe Edge as he had outlasted Democratic foe Edison.

There were reasons to believe that Hagueism had suffered more severe wounds than appeared on the surface. For the first, the Jersey city mayor and Hudson county boss was confronted with one hos-tile state administration immediately following an-other. Never before had he lacked cordial rela-tions with the chief executive's office for more than three years at a stretch. Moreover, and more serious, there loomed the threat of revision and modernization of the 1844 state constitution, an antiquated document to which Hagueism has al-ways been geared.

The successful sponsorship of a referendum au-thorizing the legislature to draw up a new consti-tution and submit it to the voters at the November, 1944, election had been Governor Edison's final, and most damaging blow at the sources of the Jersey City mayor's power. Only time, and the degree of the new governor's zest for battle, could tell how serious the blow would prove.

Frank Hague, the boss of governors, senators and judges, grew up as a problem child in one of the toughest areas of the sordid and uninspiring city across the Hudson River from New York. He was expelled from school as incorrigible after reaching the sixth grade. Before he was able to vote he had become a valuable ward heeler of the Jersey City Democratic machine. In 1908 he entered City Hall as head janitor, at $2,000 a year. Ten years later he was mayor, and through his control of the big Hudson County vote, the leader of the Democratic Party in the state.

Hague elected his first governor in 1919 after getting him nominated in a primary election which a legislative committee described as "a saturnalia of crime," in which the election laws were "violated with impunity" in Hudson County. This was only the first of many occasions on which Hague's election methods were to be similarly castigated.

The new governor, Edward I. Edwards, began the long process of appointing Hague men to the boards and commissions which run most of the state's business, and to the courts and prosecutors' offices which administer "Jersey justice" to the boss' liking. First of all, Edwards grabbed for

Hague the highway commission, which spent half of the state's budget virtually without supervision and which constituted a politician's dream of patronage, both in jobs and contracts.

The business of grafting Hagueism into the organic structure of the state was stepped up after A. Harry Moore, the boss' Jersey City pal and obedient political servant, was elected as governor in 1925 for the first of his three terms. New Jersey governors cannot succeed themselves, but Hague, who had every reason to be pleased with Moore's services, re-elected him, after a single intervening term in each case, in 1931 and 1937.

In the 1919 primary fight, in which he ousted James R. Nugent as state boss, Hague had been able to carry Hudson County by only 22,000 votes. Three years later all intra-party opposition had been crushed, and Hague was able to deliver his county by a Democratic majority of 79,905 on election day. In 1925 he pushed the election day margin up to 103,000 votes, a figure which he was able to maintain, with minor variations, from that time on.

Hague's firmly controlled 100,000-vote pluralities in Hudson County became his club for bludgeoning the state party into submission, his instrument for substantially controlling the state, and his passport into the highest political society. And Hague grew steadily more arrogant, bullying and dictatorial—and, of course, steadily more wealthy.

He acquired an apartment house in Jersey City in which he set aside a 14-room, $7,000-a-year duplex apartment for himself, and a summer show place on the beach at Deal. He inaugurated his custom of spending his winters in Florida, governing Jersey City by long distance telephone through his deputy mayor, John Malone, and his nephew, secretary and political heir, Frank Hague Eggers. He increased his already substantial bets on the races and, when the occasion arose, made Jersey City the home and sanctuary of the nation's biggest hand book horse race betting syndicate.

Hague cut a wide swathe, while Jersey City became yearly a more depressing city of dilapidated slums, broken streets, inflated assessments and high taxes.

About the only thing that was kept up-to-date, well polished and oiled, working 365 days in the year, was the mayor's formidable and dependable vote-getting organization. Its agents were to be found in every police and fire station, in the hospitals and schools, on the bench and in the jury box, in the bar association and in the chamber of commerce. On election day the machine saw to it that Hague subjects went to the polls—and voted right.

The actual running of the machine took little of Hague's time. Malone and Eggers directed its operations from City Hall, with the legal advice of John Milton and City Counsel Charles Hershenstein. Surrogate John H. Gavin and County Supervisor John F. O'Neil were members of the general staff. Judge Louis N. Paladeau served as liaison man between the boss and his legislative forces at Trenton.

The ward oragnizations were in the competent hands of such subordinates as Sheriff Parle, Tax Commissioner and ex-Sheriff John J. Coppinger, City Clerk Eugene Ertle, City Commissioner Barney Johnson, and Freeholder Patrick J. Donnelly. The city or county salaries—$6,000 to $11,000 a year—paid to these and other ward leaders, depended on their effective political activity and unquestioning personal obedience to the boss' orders, whether delivered in person or transmitted from Miami, Paris or Honolulu.

Control of the Democratic organization in Hudson County carried with it, almost automatically, the state leadership of the party, since there is no other comparable Democratic stronghold in the state.

The upper-middle-class commuter vote in the suburban towns near New York is strongly Republican. So is the country vote in the southern part of the state. Republican machines control the vote in the South Jersey cities of Camden, where the GOP organization usually has been allied with the Vare-Grundy-Pew machine in Philadelphia, dan in Atlantic City, where Enoch L. "Nucky" Johnson ruled as boss for thirty years, before he was sent to the Federal penitentiary in 1941.

"Nucky" ran his resort city in a high, wide and handsome manner, with the aid of ballot-box stuffing, padded registrations and the importation of "floaters" from Philadelphia. He provided a convenient subject of counter-attack for Hague candidates accused of subservience to "machine rule," up to the time that he was convicted of defrauding the government of $38,000 in income taxes. At the trial it developed that his income had included a regular payment of $1,200 a week from policy gamblers.

A rotten borough system of representation in the legislature, and particularly in the state Senate, always has prevented the Democrats from even coming close to controlling the legislative branch of the government. The Senate is composed of one member from each of the twenty-one counties, which range in population from Essex' 837,340 and Hudson's 652,040, down to Sussex's 29,632 and Cape May's 28,919. Of the twenty-one senators, the Democrats can never hope to have more than six or seven. (Since 1940 they have had three.)

But while Hague never controlled the legislature, he experienced little difficulty with that body. Through his control over state patronage, including the high-paying jobs to which most of the legislators aspired, he always was able to negotiate working alliances with members of the Republican majority.

Hague became something of a national issue during 1937 and 1938 because of his campaign to smash the CIO in Hudson County and his efforts, through his control of the police, the prosecutor's office and the courts, to close Jersey City to labor organizers and liberals. The Department of Justice intervened. Finally, Federal Judge William C. Clark issued an injunction curbing some of the mayor's more flagrant violations of the civil liberties of free speech, free assembly and the free press. The Clark decision had a curious sequel, which, in some ways, marked the zenith of Hague's personal and arrogant rule over New Jersey.

In June, 1938, President Roosevelt elevated Judge Clark to the Circuit Court of Appeals, an action which pleased the anti-Hague crusaders and which, at the same time, created a vacancy in the Federal District Court in Hague's political province. For that vacancy Hague recommended the appointment of T. G. Walker, a former assemblyman from Hudson County who had been rewarded for faithful service to the boss by being placed on the bench of the state's highest court, the Court of Errors and Appeals.

As it later developed, Hague had another candidate in mind for Walker's place on the state bench.

President Roosevelt delayed filling the Federal court vacancy, and, in February, 1939, Governor Moore transferred Walker from the Court of Errors and Appeals to the Hudson County Common Pleas Court, a less important post, but one which Walker readily accepted. And to the vacancy thus created on the state's highest court, Governor Moore appointed Frank Hague, Jr., the boss' son. Ten months later, when the lines were forming for the 1940 presidential campaign, President Roosevelt finally filled the Clark vacancy on the Federal court bench. He appointed T. G. Walker.

The selection of Frank Hague, Jr., for the Court of Errors and Appeals raised a fearful rumpus in New Jersey, which by then had become acutely conscious of the reputation Hagueism was giving throughout the country to "Jersey justice."

Junior's qualifications for the bench were doubtful, to put it mildly. He had failed to graduate from either of the law schools he had attended, Princeton and the University of Virginia. The circumstances under which he had passed the New Jersey bar examination raised suspicion in some minds. The Hudson County Bar Association promptly and enthusiastically gave its approval to Governor Moore's nomination of young Hague for the bench, but indignation was the most noticeable reaction in other sections of the bar. Frederic R.

Colie, a member of the Newark Bar Association, and a Republican, assumed the leadership of a spirited fight to block confirmation of the appointment by the state Senate. But within two weeks the Senate gave its approval—six Hague Republicans voting with seven Democrats to produce the necessary majority—and Junior took his place on the bench of the state's highest court.

Charles Edison, son of Thomas A. Edison, was serving as Assistant Secretary of the Navy, on leave of absence from his job as president of the Thomas A. Edison Industries, when President Roosevelt, preparing to run for a third term, looked around for a good gubernatorial candidate to help him carry the doubtful state of New Jersey. The presidential choice fell on Edison, and Hague gave his approval.

Hagueism in 1940 permeated the whole political, business, social, religious and professional life of Jersey City and, in a lesser degree, of the state. It had reached into the churches, which shared in Hague's patronage through the appointment of generously paid city and county chaplains. It had infiltrated the bar associations, professional societies and civic organizations, providing protection for the boss against the possibility of any militant opposition from those groups. By the use of jobs and favors on the one hand, and threats, strong-arm tactics and court persecutions on the other, it had bought or wrecked all organized opposition. It had split the Republican Party in the state into Hague (Hoffman) Republicans and anti-Hague Republicans. And so much hue and cry had been raised against its methods that Hagueism could no longer be ignored.

Candidate Edison, running for the governorship with Hague's support, handled the Hague issue cautiously, but clearly enough to indicate, if his words could be taken at face value, the course he actually intended to pursue. In his acceptance speech he promised that if he were elected, he would be the real governor. In a campaign speech in Hudson County, he promised that he would redeem the name of "Jersey justice," which was becoming the butt of vaudeville jokes.

Hague didn't worry too much about these and similar campaign utterances. Doubtless he felt that he could deal with any situation that might arise. On election day, President Roosevelt swept Hudson County by the record-breaking vote of 280,000 to Willkie's 107,000, and Hague delivered his machine plurality of 108,000 for Edison. Roosevelt's plurality in the state was only 71,500 and Edison's was 64,000. Each owed his victory in the state to Boss Hague.

When Governor Edison took office in January, succeeding A. Harry Moore, his first action was to rip out of the executive office the private telephone wire from Jersey City, by which Hague had been running the state. The Jersey City mayor shrugged this off as a meaningless gesture. But a few days later Governor Edison drew blood.

A vacancy had occurred on the state Supreme Court bench through the retirement of Justice Trenchard, who had presided at the trial of Richard Hauptmann in the Lindberg kidnapping case. Mayor Hague was ready with his candidate for the job the minute Trenchard's resignation was handed in. From Miami he telephoned Arthur Walsh, the governor's business associate and campaign manager (later appointed to the United States Senate by Edison), to recommend a man whose "vote," Hague assured Walsh, "you can depend on in a pinch." The suggestion was entirely characteristic of Hague's approach to the subject of judicial appointments.

Several days went by and then Governor Edison announced that he intended to appoint, of all people, Frederic R. Colie, the Newark lawyer who had led the fight against the appointment of Frank Hague, Jr., two years earlier.

By telephone from Miami, Hague protested bitterly to Edison. "I'm going to break you, Charlie, if it's the last thing I do," he wound up, "because you're a damned ingrate."

Edison went through with the Colie nomination, and the fat was in the fire.

The governor next turned his attention to the State Highway Department, a rich patronage claim which was being worked jointly by Hague and the Republican majority in the state legislature. The highway commissioner is appointed by the governor, with the advice and consent of the Senate, for a term of six years. During his term he submits his budget requests directly to the legislature, and operates entirely independently of the chief executive. As it happened, the term of the commissioner, E. Donald Sterner, expired four months after Edison's inauguration.

As Sterner's successor, Edison selected William L. Dill, who twice had been an unsuccessful Democratic candidate for governor, and who had held various appointive offices in the state. The nomination precipitated a sit-down strike in the state Senate. Under the constitution, Sterner was entitled to continue in office until his successor was appointed and confirmed. It took Governor Edison a full year, and the threat of an investigation of the highway department, to rout Commissioner Sterner out of the office.

In the meantime, the Edison-Hague feud had broken out into the open, with both principals issuing heated statements, charges and counter-charges. The open break was precipitated by Edison's railroad tax compromise, which the legislature approved despite Hague's opposition.

Mayor Hague had performed many services for New Jersey's big industries, individually and collectively, not the least of them being his campaign to drive the CIO out of the state. But the mayor had fastened on the $34,000,000, plus interest, owed by the railroads in back taxes, as his special talking point to prove his devotion to the people's interest. Hague didn't collect the taxes—that would have destroyed the issue. He just talked about them, vowing that the railroads would never be allowed to escape payment.

The tax debt had accumulated during the period of railroad bankruptcy and reorganization in the depression. Under Edison's compromise settlement, the railroads agreed to pay the $34,000,000 in principal over periods ranging up to twenty years, while the state waived $24,000,000 in accumulated interest.

Hague's legislators fought ratification of the compromise. The mayor himself denounced the settlement and its author, Governor Edison, in statements, speeches and in full page newspaper advertisements. Edison replied: "Mayor Hague is trying with calculated abuse to pay me off for the appointment of Justice Frederic R. Colie to the New Jersey Supreme Court."

A few days after the tax compromise was approved by the legislature, Hague announced that he was relinquishing the state leadership of the

Democratic Party and conferring it on Governor
Edison who, he observed, henceforth would have
to "stand on his two feet."

Edison's comment was that the party leadership
was not Hague's to confer; that that power resided
only in the Democratic voters of the state. But the
governor showed no hesitancy about standing on
his own feet.

President Roosevelt picked this stage of the New
Jersey squabble to indicate his approval of Hague
by nominating Thomas F. Meany, a Hague career
lawyer, to fill a vacancy on the Federal district
court bench in New Jersey. Edison unhesitatingly
joined in a widespread appeal to the Senate Judiciary Committee to reject the nomination.

"The people," he testified before the committee,
"will always be dubious of the quality of justice
obtainable from a judge who all his life has been
a part of, and obligated to, a sordid political machine." Hague's congresswoman, Mary T. Norton,
also appeared before the committee. She described
the New Jersey governor as "the most arrant hypo-
crite that ever walked in New Jersey."

Edison's next move was to strike directly at the
financial sources of Hague's power in Jersey City
and Hudson County.

During its long reign the machine had loaded
down Hague's city with a tremendous superstruc-
ture of patronage and high-cost government. The

tax rate had climbed to a record level of $57.45 per $1,000, and, in addition, the assessment rolls had been padded and overinflated. In an effort to obtain relief, the City Affairs Committee of Jersey City filed with Governor Edison charges of dereliction of duty against the three Democrats and two Republicans who constituted the Hudson County Tax Board.

In the executive trial which followed, and which the governor conducted, it was disclosed that while most property owners were paying taxes on inflated assessments, some big corporations, favored financial institutions and newspapers, were grossly under-assessed. The Prudential Life Insurance Company, represented by former state Senator Edward P. Stout, a Hague lieutenant, fared better than most of the other companies.

Governor Edison threw out the whole Hudson County Tax Board and substituted one of his own selection. The new board proceeded to reduce assessments on 34,000 pieces of property by $96,-000,000. But it raised the assessment of the *Jersey City Journal* from $50,000 to $200,000.

Hague fought back in typical fashion.

Leo Rosenblum, associate counsel for the City Affairs Committee in its action against the Hague tax board, had been appointed by Edison as president of the new board. Soon after he took office, Rosenblum was arrested and indicted in Jersey

City on what proved to be a trumped up charge of evading the Selective Service Act. The indictment was nolle prossed and Rosenblum, entirely exonerated, filed libel suits against those responsible for making the charges.

The chief counsel for the City Affairs Committee in the tax board proceedings was former Judge John Warren, of Jersey City. Not long after the disposal of the case, a $150,000 suit, involving the ownership of a mortgage, was filed against Warren in the Jersey City Chancery Court. Warren termed the suit an instrument of blackmail and revenge. He appealed to the Court of Errors and Appeals to take the action out of the hands of the Chancery Court, which Warren said everybody knew was "absolutely dominated by Frank Hague and used by him for his personal and political purposes." One of the members of the high court, before whom this plea for relief was laid, was Frank Hague, Jr.

In his warfare with Edison, Hague repeatedly used his control over the law enforcement agencies of Hudson County to strike back at the governor's allies and instruments. Early in the new governor's term, James J. Donovan, then mayor and director of public safety of Bayonne, a city in Hudson County, broke with Hague and joined forces with Edison. After a brief period of preparation, Hague's county prosecutor, Daniel O'Reagan, sent squads of detectives into Bayonne and raided a series of taverns. Scores of persons were arrested, held for days as material witnesses, and questioned by O'Reagan and members of his staff. With the evidence thus gathered, Hague's prosecutor obtained indictments against Donovan and several members of his official family for non-feasance in office. The charge against Mayor Donovan was that he had failed to clean up vice in Bayonne.

But the most celebrated instance of what has been called Hague's "persecution" of his political foes concerns the case of John R. Longo. The story goes back to 1937.

In that year, Longo, then twenty-four years old, and ambitious, started a campaign to build himself up as a rival for Mayor Hague's political crown in Hudson County. He organized an anti-Hague slate of county candidates and entered it in the Democratic primary. Hague could not have been worried by Longo's puny challenge, but he obviously didn't like to have a precedent established for county-wide primary fights. Most bosses, in that situation, would have given Longo a small job and shut him up. Hague had him arrested.

Longo was indicted for filing fraudulent primary petitions, a laughable charge to anyone familiar with the casual method in which petitions normally are prepared in the party clubhouses. He was convicted by a Hague jury and given an exemplary sentence of nine months in the penitentiary by a Hague judge. But that was only the beginning of the Longo story.

He popped up again in 1940 as an employe of the Hudson County elections bureau during a brief and abortive push by anti-Hague Republicans to clean up the voting lists in Jersey City. Superintendent of Elections William E. Sewell, who had been put in that office by the legislature to purge the registration lists, hired Longo as one of his assistants. Hague lawyers and judges defended the Jersey City voting lists savagely. Sewell's ardor soon cooled off, and Longo resigned his job.

In February, 1943, when Governor Edison's supreme bid for party control was getting under way, Longo was appointed deputy clerk of Hudson County. This was an affront that Hague could not let pass. This time he was charged with having altered his voting record, while an employe of the election bureau, to make it appear that he voted as a Democrat, rather than as a Republican.

Again Longo was convicted and sentenced; this time to a prison term of eighteen months to three years. After the trial, Longo's attorney discovered, it was alleged, that the prosecutor had suppressed vital evidence which would have proved Longo's innocence; also that six state witnesses had given perjured testimony. The defense attorney called the case against Longo "the most outrageous frame-up in the annals of Hudson County." Governor Edison expressed the opinion that Longo was being persecuted. The City Affairs Committee of Jersey City, which had sponsored the tax assessment reforms, appealed to Department of Justice in Washington to step into Hague's city and put an end to Hague's "persistent suppresion of civil rights."

The committee's petition to the United States Attorney General said: "We are confident that the reputed influence of Mayor Hague in Washington will not deter a full and complete prosecution by your department . . ." Not everyone shared the committee's confidence. Hague himself, rooting vociferously for a fourth term for President Roosevelt, seemed unworried.

Governor Edison's underlying purpose in all of his moves against Hague had been so to weaken the Jersey city boss by loss of state patronage and city funds, and by breaking up his alliances throughout the state, that Edison finally could win the party control which Hague had once pretended to give him. A significant step in this campaign was the governor's appointment of state Senator Crawford Jamieson, of Trenton, to a $12,000-a-year post on the public utilities commission. Jamieson had been regarded for years as the leader of the anti-Hague wing of the Democratic Party.

In a preliminary test of strength at the 1942

state convention the Hague forces demonstrated that they still had full control. The mayor's political lieutenants were put in all key positions. The convention voted to ignore in the party platform the question of revision of the state constitution, which was one of Edison's main objectives. In the campaign which followed, Governor Edison refused to support United States Senator William H. Smathers, the Democratic candidate for re-election, and Smathers was defeated by his Republican opponent, Albert Hawkes.

With the opening of the final year of the governor's term, the battle for party control got under way in earnest. Edison's aim was to win control of the state committee in the September primary.

Dramatically, the governor announced (January 31, 1943) that he had formed a political alliance with Mayor Bernard McFeeley, of Hoboken. McFeeley had always been a strong Hague supporter and the leader of one of the major wings of the Hague organization. He had been under attack from reform elements almost as consistently as had Hague himself.

The basis for the Edison-McFeeley alliance had been created fortuitously by the death of Hudson County Clerk Gustav Back. After a conference with the Hoboken mayor, Edison announced that he would fill the vacancy by appointing William H. Gilfert, of Hoboken, as county clerk. And to make perfectly clear the meaning of the step, he added that Gilfert would name John R. Longo, Hague's old Jersey City foe, as his deputy.

"Mayor McFeeley and Gilfert," said Edison, "have promised me wholehearted support in the fight to bring democracy back to Hudson County. I am pleased to have their assistance."

(Longo's second arrest and conviction, already described, followed promptly after his induction into office.)

In February, Edison's state-wide campaign organization, "United Democracy," came into being at a dinner in Trenton. Representatives of all sections of the state, including most of the Democrats who had been appointed to office by Edison, were present. Secretary of State Joseph A. Brophy was elected chairman of the organization. Governor Edison opened the organization's headquarters, and the primary campaign, with a speech in which he called for a reaffirmation of the "liberal and progressive" policies of Thomas Jefferson.

A few weeks later he took to the radio to denounce Hagueism in stinging terms. He dared its leader to run for governor and thus give the voters an opportunity to approve or reject his "philosophy of dictatorship." Mayor Hague, he asserted, was notorious all over the United States as the epitome of the "what-do-I-get-out-of-it school of politics" and as one who had "ruthlessly crushed or corrupted all opposition to his personal ambitions."

There was nothing new in that, and Hague and Hagueism had long since become inured to mere words. The mayor was concentrating on the tangible issues of the retention of party control in the primary and the election of a governor who would undo the damage wrought by Edison. Hague assured his subordinates during the Spring that A. Harry Moore, reliable both as a vote-getter and as a chief executive, would go into office as Edison's successor, and that all would be well. But when the time came for the showdown, Hague discovered that his supposed ace-in-the-hole was only a deuce.

For about a year, Mayor Vincent J. Murphy, of Newark, a former plumber, officer of the plumbers' union, and, since 1931, secretary-treasurer of the politically potent New Jersey State Federation of Labor, had been warming up for a possible race for governor. On the evening of July 27, when the deadline for primary filing was approaching, a delegation of state labor leaders called on Mayor Hague and notified him that they would not support Moore for the Democratic nomination. The next morning Hague regretfully disclosed to the state that Moore's health would not permit him to run. Almost simultaneously, Edison announced that he would support Murphy for the nomination. And two hours later Hague, completely outgeneraled, also, reluctantly, came out for Murphy.

The boss had been outsmarted. But with his 100,000 Hudson County plurality in his pocket, he was far from beaten.

Two months earlier, aided by the hoopla attending his anti-Hague campaign, Governor Edison had succeeded finally in putting through the legislature a bill which provided for a referendum at the 1943 election on his proposal for modernizing the state constitution. The question on which the people were to vote was whether or not the next legislature should be authorized to rewrite the basic law. Edison, of course, favored adoption of the referendum proposal, while Hague opposed it.

A second issue between the governor and the boss was the railroad tax compromise. Hague had opened a campaign for repeal of the law by which the compromise had been given effect.

Caught in the middle between his two chief supporters, candidate Murphy attempted to mollify them both by coming out, gingerly, for constitutional revision and, cautiously, for repeal of the railroad tax law.

The September primary, at which delegates to the state convention were elected, resulted in a decisive victory for Boss Hague and a crushing defeat for Edison's "United Democracy." The convention, completely controlled by Hague, met early in October and adopted a state platform which demanded repeal of Edison's railroad tax compromise. The party platform said nothing at all on the subject of constitutional revision.

Candidate Murphy found sitting on the fence between the warring Hague and Edison factions too difficult a balancing feat for one of his limited political accomplishments. As the campaign against Republican candidate Walter E. Edge progressed, he slipped by imperceptible stages definitely into the Hague camp. By election day, Murphy had quit mentioning constitutional revision in his speeches. Hague, outmaneuvered at the start of the campaign, had rectified matters by stealing Edison's candidate. He had no reason to doubt that he could control Murphy. But the problem of electing him still remained.

Edison acknowledged the new situation by dropping all mention of the Democratic candidate for governor from his campaign speeches. In his election eve speech, Edison appealed solely for a favorable vote on the constitutional revision referendum.

Mayor Hague, the governor said, "fears, and with reason, that his ruthless practices will be stopped and his arbitrary power ended if a new constitution is adopted." And as his final contribution to the campaign, Edison noted that the Jersey City mayor and Democratic state boss was "a man who makes Jerseymen, wherever they go in this nation, blush and apologize for their state."

Hague was finding himself in rather strange company for a man who only a few years before had run liberals and labor leaders out of the state. CIO President Philip Murray and Sidney Hillman, chairman of the CIO's political action committee, pitched into the battle to help elect Murphy. The Communist New York *Daily Worker* not only urged Murphy's election; it found some kind words to say for Boss Hague himself.

Hague welcomed support from all quarters. Hudson County, he promised, would give the Democratic candidate a plurality of 100,000 votes. And with that nucleus to work on, he warned, it was up to Murphy's labor backers to do the job in the rest of the state.

Hague delivered, but the labor groups didn't.

Murphy carried Hudson County by 96,431, but was snowed under by a majority of 224,439 in the rest of the state, making a net majority of 128,008 for Edge. Constitutional revision was beaten by 87,289 in Hudson County, but approved by a majority of 223,641 in the rest of the state, for a net favorable majority of 136,352.

Hague had been overwhelmed on both counts, but an analysis of the vote showed a degree of machine control of the voting in Hudson County that was little short of perfection. The total vote in New Jersey had reached a peak of 1,961,280 in the 1940 presidential election. In the state outside of Hudson County the vote for governor in 1943 was less than half as large—46 per cent—but with the Hague machine at work in Hudson County the total vote fell only 30 per cent from the 1940 high.

Comparison of the total vote for governor with the total vote on constitutional revision gave even more striking proof of the machine's effectiveness. With Hudson County excluded, only 49 per cent of those who voted for candidates for governor bothered to vote on the constitutional revision referendum. But in Hague's county, 80 per cent of all those who voted for governor also recorded their preference for or against constitutional revision. And, finally, the anti-Hague vote in favor of constitutional revision in Hudson County was 30 per cent below the anti-Hague vote for Edge for governor; while the predominantly machine-controlled vote against revision was only 17 per cent below the vote for Murphy for governor. Making allowance for the uncontrolled portion of Murphy's support, this indicated virtually a 100 per cent performance by the Hague machine.

Hagueism was under heavy fire as the new Republican administration was inaugurated in the state. It faced the uncharted perils of a new state constitution. But on its own home grounds, Hague seemed to be as strongly entrenched as ever.

5

BAY STATE, STREAMLINED

So GRADUALLY that it has escaped notice, a brand
new model of a political machine has been
developed in Massachusetts during the past two
decades.

The new model is prosaically labeled, "Massachusetts Republican State Committee." It has the
conventional parts, but it is highly streamlined and
equipped with some interesting new gadgets that
make for better central control and smoother operation, and some that are designed to prevent knock-
ing and to reduce friction to a minimum. It has
been tried out for some time now, and it works.

How much the impressiveness of the new machine is due to contrast with the Democratic machine clattering away on the other side of the
street would be hard to say. Undoubtedly some
of it. The Democratic contraption is a broken-

down, worn-out Model T Irish political machine into which so many monkey wrenches have been thrown that it is no longer recognizable. Its parts have fallen off or been flung off. It has been patched up and repainted countless times; that it runs at all seems to be due mostly to habit.

Nowhere in the country has the break-up of boss rule left greater political chaos than in Massachusetts Democracy, a bit of the "ould sod" which is fully living up to the tradition that the Irish would rather fight each other than unite against a common enemy. And in no state have the Republicans shown more skill in taking full advantage of the opportunity thus presented.

Until the late twenties Boston was dominated by two strong Democratic machines and a group of subsidiary ward machines. The all-powerful machines were the Hendricks Club of the old Eighth Ward, for forty years the personal political property of "Czar" Martin Lomasney; and Boston's Tammany Club, which produced the fabulous James M. "Jim" Curley and served as his vehicle to temporary dominance of the state.

Both organizations were typical big-city ward machines. They helped the poor and befriended the unfortunate. In Lomasney's case, recipients of his favors and largess paid off in votes, never in money—something that hasn't been equally true of latter-day Democratic politics in Boston, where a sheriff and a court clerk were jailed in 1942 for selling jobs.

The Tammany Club, according to general repute, wasn't always as scrupulous as was Lomasney about the sources of its financial support, and charges of fraudulent voting were more likely to center in its bailiwick.

Lomasney's power in city and state affairs came from his absolute sway over the old Eighth Ward, (now Ward 3) and from his strategic generalship in using that control as a balance of power in city elections. It was Lomasney's custom to wait until the Sunday before election before announcing his position in city and state primary contests. The delay gave him an opportunity to assess the situation, and also served to build up an atmosphere of suspense, with nervous candidates seeking his backing and with the newspapers contributing their speculation about which way Lomasney would go.

When the strategic Sunday arrived, thousands of second generation members of immigrant families, who had moved from the "Czar's" precincts in the North and West Ends but who still regarded Lomasney as their leader, would return to visit with the old folk and to listen to their boss' advice on candidates.

Lomasney's endorsement of a city-wide candidate carried with it the solid vote of his ward and at least 10,000 votes throughout the rest of the city.

Usually, that was enough to swing the balance. For himself, the boss was content with perpetual service in the state legislature and with his power to pick judges, aldermen, congressmen and frequently mayors. But even before Lomasney's death, machine politics was losing its grip on Boston.

The fatal blow to the city machines, as such, was struck by the Republican state legislature when it forced upon Boston a system of non-partisan election of mayors. The provision for an open primary, with party labels barred, followed by a run-off between the two top men in the general election, had the effect of wiping out party lines and promoting factional, rather than party, strife. More than that, it frequently operated to give the Republican minority in Boston the power to pick the mayor by uniting behind one of the Democratic candidates.

(The most recent city election, when an overwhelming majority of Republicans voted for Maurice Tobin, enabling him to defeat "Jim" Curley by less than 10,000 majority, was an example.)

The effect of the non-partisan city elections was felt throughout the party organization. Party patronage in the city administration gradually was replaced by an award of spoils along personal and factional lines. The influence of the Democratic

City Committee shrank almost to nothing. The ward committees, which had been composed of active party workers and vote getters, were so weakened that in most wards they finally were reduced to merely nominal existence.

Although these effects were beginning to make themselves felt in his latter years, Lomasney continued to wield a considerable influence up to the time of his death. After 1932 his political empire completely fell apart in a series of factional struggles among his chief lieutenants, none of whom was big enough to step into the boss' shoes. But some of Lomasney's chief aides managed to do very well for themselves in the scramble.

John P. Higgins, one of the group, supported Charles P. Hurley for governor of Massachusetts and, after Hurley's election, made a brief pretense to the party leadership of Boston. But as Higgins was preparing to run for mayor, the death of the chief justice of the Superior Civil Court in Suffolk County opened an opportunity he could not resist. Governor Hurley appointed Higgins to the bench post, taking him out of the mayoralty race. Although his judicial robes technically keep him out of the hurly-burly of party politics, Chief Justice Higgins has continued to wield considerable influence in Boston's faction-torn Democracy.

John I. Fitzgerald, known to his colleagues as

"John I.," to distinguish him from Boston's many other politically inclined Fitzgeralds, was Lomasney's principal lieutenant and successor as head of the Hendricks Club. He did not fare so well. His defeat in 1943 for a seat in the Boston City Council put the final period to the story of the effective life of the Hendricks Club.

Boston's Tammany Club, meanwhile, was going through a similar decline, but it left more of an impression on the city's politics because of the continuing prominence of several of its former members.

"Jim" Curley ranks first on the list. Former governor, three times mayor, ex-alderman, and in 1944 member of Congress, Curley has been a vivid figure in Massachusetts politics for forty years. He is a heavy and lucky gambler, possessor of a glib tongue, but a sucker for Wall Street speculation. Curley has made several fortunes, only to lose them in the stock market or in wildcat promotion schemes.

Another product of the Tammany Club, protege of Curley, and his one-time secretary, is the present mayor of Boston, Maurice Tobin.

It was out of the Tammany Club that the latest futile attempt to re-establish machine rule in Boston came, within the past few years. Michael A. Ward, another Curley pupil and one-time secretary, became one of the leading figures in the club after Curley moved out of the district. Ward went into the contracting business and, on the side, won election successively to the state legislature, the City Council, and, finally, to the City School Committee, of which he is now a member. Ward eventually moved to the Brighton section of the city, bought a building in which he founded the Jackson Democratic Club, and proceeded to turn Brighton from a Republican to a Democratic district.

Encouraged by this success, he conceived the idea of organizing Jackson Clubs in other wards with the idea of making himself eventually boss of the Democratic organization throughout the city. The political soil was not fertile for the growth of his scheme, however, and he found himself opposed by all the other local leaders.

Representative John J. McCormack, administration leader of the lower house of Congress, announced that he was opposed to machine politics in any form and that he would fight to keep Ward out of his section. Ward finally abandoned the idea, but he remained one of the few local leaders able to deliver anything like a machine vote in his district.

The Boston ward leaders, on the whole, are of negligible importance in present-day politics. The Democratic City Committee, which they comprise, is equally impotent. The city chairman, Billy "Mother" Galvin (so called because of his motherly voice) has no control over his unruly subordinates. Galvin ran a speakeasy during prohibition days. His political importance now is recognized by his occupancy of the civil service job of superintendent of markets, to which he was appointed by Mayor Tobin.

In recent years the Massachusetts Democracy has looked less like a party than a free-for-all. Here are some things that happen when the Bay State's Irish Democrats pay their respects to one another:

1. Joseph B. Ely, former Democratic governor, called ex-Governor and ex-Mayor Curley a "polecat."

2. Majority Leader John J. McCormack of the United States House of Representatives and William J. Foley, district attorney of Suffolk County (Boston), don't speak to each other.

3. Attorney General Paul A. Dever, as 1940 candidate for governor, spurned the aid of Lieutenant Governer Francis Kelly, who had polled 100,000 votes against him in a primary fight for the nomination; then regretted it on election day, when he lost to Republican candidate Leverett Saltonstall by only 5,588 votes.

4. Michael A. Ward, potent Democratic leader in the Brighton section of Boston, supported Republican Senator Henry Cabot Lodge for re-election in 1942 and so earned the description (by

Representative McCormack) of a "renegade Dem-crat."

5. And Massachusetts is the place where Tom Buckley and Francis X. Hurley, both previously unknown in politics (Buckley was a WPA work-er), succeeded in being nominated and elected to state office by capitalizing on the Irish habit of voting for familiar names.

The main cleavage in Boston and Massachusetts Democracy has been along pro- and anti-Roosevelt lines, but the lines have been complicated and more deeply etched by bitter local feuds and rival per-sonal ambitions. In some cases these have sprung from the ideological division over the New Deal; in others, existing personal feuds were the main factors in determining the lineup on national issues.

State Treasurer Francis X. Hurley is friendly with former President Hoover, and actively sup-ported Wendell L. Willkie in the 1940 campaign. Boston's District Attorney Foley followed him into the Willkie camp. Former Governor Ely bolted the New Deal with New York's Alfred E. Smith, and has "taken a walk" on so many election days that he is hardly recognized as a Democrat when he returns briefly to the fold. Joseph P. Ken-nedy, former Ambassador to Great Britain, has thrown in his fortunes with the President's polit-ical foes.

Early in 1944 the formation of the Thomas Jefferson Forum, Inc., was announced by Bernard J. Killion, a prominent Boston lawyer. Massachusetts Democrats recognized that Representative McCormack, a close friend of Killion, was its real political sponsor and that the organization represented an attempt to unify the party for the presidential campaign.

Its backers hoped to enlist in the Thomas Jefferson Forum, Inc., a membership of two to three hundred prominent non-office holding Democrats who would be able and willing to make substantial contributions to the party's campaign fund. Thus well heeled, they hoped that the new organization would be able to wield a dominant influence over a regular party organization which seemed both politically and financially bankrupt.

II

During the period of increasing Democratic chaos, a Republican state organization was evolving along lines of businesslike efficiency which have not usually been considered adaptable to the handling of the human raw materials out of which votes and party loyalties are fabricated.

The groundwork for the new organization was laid between 1922 and 1925, when Joseph W. Martin served as the executive secretary of the Republican State Committee his efficiency being vital.

"Joe" Martin, a born compromiser and conciliator, already had fully developed the personal qualities which later enabled him, as Republican Minority Leader of the House of Representatives, to lead two factions of the party despite the fact that they seemed frequently to be headed in opposite directions. His method of leadership, demonstrated also as Republican National Chairman during and after Wendell L. Willkie's 1940 presidential campaign, was to scurry rapidly back and forth among the principal factions of his followers, attempting, not without some success, to create the illusion that his flock was just one big happy family.

With "Joe" handling the business of the Massachusetts State Committee, the principle that the organization should not take any part in intra-party strife, but should devote its energies solely to the effort to elect any candidate bearing the Republican label in November, became firmly established in the party's tradition. The result was to divorce the state committee from all controversial questions of statesmanship and personalities, and to limit its activities strictly to raising funds and building the party organization.

When "Joe" Martin moved on to Congress in 1925, the Republican bosses of Massachusetts passed over the field of politicians to put these activities in the hands of a man who was an expert at them. As executive secretary of the State Committee they hired Charles E. Nichols, who had been efficient and productive as the secretary of the wealthy and powerful Associated Industries of Massachusetts. They gave Nichols a handsome salary and what amounted to civil service tenure. Since 1925, state chairmen have come and gone, but Nichols has remained as the functioning mainspring of the State Committee.

The new executive secretary looked over the material he had to work with, and found it not too good. Like every other political organization, the Massachusetts Republican machine was encumbered with dozens of tired, superannuated leaders who no longer were able or willing to work at the job, but who couldn't be tossed out arbitrarily without alienating them, their friends and any casual voters who might still regard the oldsters as statesmen.

Nichols, no doubt, would have liked to do what he had done for the Associated Industries: throw out the inefficient non-producers and install a live organizer in every community. That he didn't try anything of the sort proved the wisdom that had been shown in his selection. But through the years, as opportunity offered, and within the limits set by the nature of politics, Nichols aided in the installation of county, district and town chairmen and field organizers whom he would have been glad to hire in similar capacities for a private business association.

The state political machine which he has built is closely integrated and subject to central direction down through all of its branches. The state committee keeps a firm grip on the party organization in every county and town through its control of finances. Funds for all party purposes are collected by the Republican Finance Committee, which operates under the state committee. These funds go into a common pot. The state, city, town and district committees all operate on expense budgets, which must be submitted to the state committee and approved by it. After the budgets are approved the funds are allocated by the state organization to all the lesser committees.

The collection of funds is as highly organized as is their disbursal. The State Finance Committee sets a quota for every local party committee, based on the size of the Republican vote in each party jurisdiction. The local committee members are encouraged to go out and solicit contributions of $.50, $1.00, $2.00 and $5.00, as well as larger sums, on the sound theory that "the voters will follow their money."

This system has greatly increased the number of contributors—from around 2,000 to nearly 20,000 —as well as the total amount collected. It also has generally stimulated all other forms of party activity.

In addition to the tight rein which it keeps all down the line through its control of party funds, the state committee maintains a close supervision over the whole organization through field chairmen and organizers. Every district, city and town committee is set up along the same lines as is the state committee itself, with sub-committees for registration, transportation (the doorbell ringers), rallies and speakers, publicity, etc., and all of them are closely knit into the state committee's framework.

The thoroughness with which all this business is conducted is illustrated by the handling of charters for Republican clubs. In order to use the party name these clubs, of which there are about 260, have to obtain a charter from the state committee. An article in the by-laws of the state committee prohibits any club chartered by the committee from taking part in primary contests. When an application for a charter for a new club is received, the Nichols organization checks up on the group seeking it. If it appears that the club has been formed to promote some individual's ambitions, the charter is denied and the club cannot use the word "Republican" in its name. This operates to reduce intra-party frictions and to increase the general year-round and, especially, election day efficiency of the whole organization, often proved.

During the past ten years the Republicans have devoted considerable effort and attention to cutting down election frauds by the various factions in Boston, where the vote still runs two-to-one Democratic. In a characteristic move, the GOP State Committee hired Pinkerton and Burns detectives to check up on fraudulent registrations and repeater voting in the 1936 election. The bill came to $10,000.

After the Republicans elected aristocratic Leverett Saltonstall as governor in 1938, the payoff in patronage was handled through the machinery of the state committee and its constituent city and town committees.

The governor, who perhaps would have preferred to select his subordinates on a less political basis, yielded to the pressure of his job-hungry supporters. With his possibly unwilling sanction, the state payrolls were purged of Democrats right down to the $15-a-week classifications.

As patronage dispenser Governor Saltonstall selected Carroll L. Meins, who had been chairman of the Boston Republican City Committee and who was a member of the GOP State Executive Committee. He installed Meins in the strategic office of president of the state department of public utilities, from which Meins filtered out state jobs through Nichols to the district, city and town chairmen.

The strengthening of the organization which resulted returned good dividends to Governor Saltonstall when he was re-elected by a 5,588-vote margin in 1940, despite President Roosevelt's plurality of 137,000 votes over Wendell L. Willkie.

Because of its complete divorcement from policy-making, the Massachusetts state machine has no hesitancy in recognizing the state's member of the National Committee as titular head of the party organization. But the Bay State has no dearth—rather a superfluity—of statesmen. No less than three of them—Governor Saltonstall, Senator Henry Cabot Lodge, and "Joe" Martin—have come to think of themselves as potential "dark horse" candidates for President or, at the very least, as good vice-presidential timber.

Through such an array of talent, National Committeeman Sinclair Weeks has had to thread his way with care. But Weeks has held his own, thanks to his ability as a collector of large campaign contributions. The Bay State's National Committeeman inherited a large fortune and wide business connections, as well as an interest in political management, from his father, John W. Weeks, a partner in the stock exchange firm of Hornblower and Weeks, and a one-time member of the United States Senate, and Secretary of War in the cabinets of Presidents Harding and Coolidge.

Sinclair Weeks attempted to follow his father's

career by seeking a seat in the Senate in 1936, but he lost the Republican nomination to young Lodge, who also had an hereditary claim to the job through his grandfather of the same name.

Even if Weeks never gets to the Senate he still may sit in his father's old chair as Secretary of War. He was one of Willkie's first boosters in 1940, and has been closely allied with the Hoosier candidate ever since then. If Willkie becomes President, Massachusetts politicians have Weeks tagged as his Secretary of War.

6

GRUNDYISM AGAIN

THERE HAVE BEEN times during the past twelve
years when it seemed that the Roosevelt revolution was about to tear Pennsylvania permanently
from the industrial feudalism which the Republican
state organization has imposed on the Keystone
State since the Civil War.

The Philadelphia city machine—Republican
counterpart of Tammany Hall—has been hanging
on the ropes more than once, although it has never
quite been knocked out.

But the worst of the storm appears to have
passed. It can now be seen that the Democratic
victories during the '30s were mere improvisations.
The Republican machine still rules. "Joe" Grundy,
with the help of "Joe" Pew's easy-flowing millions,
has re-established the Old Guard's grip on the state.
The "Joes" have made Pennsylvania safe. In the

state election of 1942 and the Philadelphia election of 1943 it became obvious that Pennsylvania was well along on the road "back to normalcy."

Republican boss rule in Pennsylvania has a long history. Since the Civil War the state has been ruled successively by Matthew S. Quay, Boies Penrose, Andrew W. Mellon and Joseph R. Grundy, with whom Joseph N. Pew, Jr., is now allied. Each of them has been many times a millionaire.

During the same eighty-year period a succession of feudal bosses, allied with the state bosses except during occasional periods of bitter warfare, has completely dominated the government of Philadelphia. The barons of Philadelphia, William B. Mann, Robert Mackey, James McManes, David Martin, Israel Durham, James P. McNichol, Boies Penrose and the Vare brothers, Edwin H. and William S., have been far more powerful, each in his turn, than any of the elected public officials whom they were accustomed to make and break.

Pennsylvania and Philadelphia have been hardened to the expenditure of tremendous amounts of money to buy elections. The state is accustomed to vote frauds on a big scale, and to repeated scandals in the misuse of public funds. Two of the men elected by the state as United States Senators—"Matt" Quay in 1898 and "Bill" Vare in 1926—have been denied seats in that body even when it was controlled by members of their own party, because of notorious graft and fraud in their elections.

Boies Penrose succeeded to the state leadership in 1904 on the death of Quay, who had ruled Pennsylvania for more than thirty years and who had developed Penrose as his heir. A Philadelphia aristocrat, graduate of Harvard, a brilliant writer, Penrose introduced a new type of leadership to the state. He had all the audacity of Quay's brazen methods of operation, but because of his social standing, education and great wealth, he was able to cover the seamier side of politics with a veneer of respectability which never entirely wore off.

Penrose was a shrewd, smooth operator. He not only dominated the Philadelphia and state machines, he introduced a new wrinkle by contributing to the support of the various anti-machine groups which arose during his time and neatly turning them to his own benefit. Penrose was capable, even, of organizing his own "reform" movements.

When the Vare brothers were on the rise in 1911, they split the party in Philadelphia in a primary fight against the established leadership of Penrose and James P. McNichol, with the result that the Republican dynasty in Philadelphia's City Hall was ousted for the first time in more than fifty years. The candidate of the Democratic and Keystone parties, Rudolph Blankerburg, "the Dutch Cleanser," became mayor for a four-year term. Penrose, too smart ever to adopt a rule or ruin policy, made peace with the Vare faction and the united Republicans elected Thomas B. Smith as mayor in 1915 by a tremendous majority. But Mayor Smith immediately cast in his lot with the Vares, whom he was able to recognize as the new and rising stars in Philadelphia politics.

Penrose's star was, indeed, fading, but he still could outwit his less experienced rivals in the long run. The "big fellow" threw his state organization into the fight to recapture City Hall and whipped up the reform groups against the Vares. In a primary fight that made history, the Penrose candidate, J. Hampton Moore, won the mayoralty nomination in 1919 from John M. Patterson, supported by the Vares, by a majority of only 1,313. It was in that 1919 fight with the Vares that Penrose, through his control over the legislature, gave Philadelphia what passed for a "reform" charter, under which the city still operates.

The Penrose charter did make some real reforms. It provided for the municipal collection of refuse, garbage and ashes, eliminating what had been one of the chief sources of municipal graft for Mc-Nichol and the Vares, whose private companies had held the contracts for those services. And it eliminated the system of private contracts (also traditionally held by the GOP bosses) for cleaning the city streets.

But under the guise of reform, the Penrose charter also altered the method of city elections so as to make it impossible for anything less than an earth-shaking and sustained uprising to upset the machine's control of the municipal government. The charter separated the city election into three parts, spread over three years. Under this system the mayor is elected one year, the controller, receiver of taxes, treasurer and county officers the next year, and the judicial candidates, who control more patronage than either the mayor or the "row officers," the third year. Penrose thus made sure that no brief and passing revolt against the machine, no matter how violent, could deprive it of control over more than one-third of the city administration. The astuteness of this scheme became fully apparent in later years.

Penrose died in 1921, early in the administration of Mayor "Hampy" Moore, and the Vares became the undisputed bosses of Philadelphia.

The state organization, in which Penrose had able lieutenants but no strong rival ready to step into his shoes, presented a picture of partial disintegration after the boss' death. Andrew W. Mellon, one of the richest men in America, a dominant figure in finance and industry, controlling the aluminum trust and scores of large oil, coal and iron companies, was able to take over the nominal leadership of the organization because of his strategic position as Secretary of the Treasury in President Harding's cabinet.

But Joseph Grundy, head of the powerful Pennsylvania Manufacturers Association, who for many years had been one of Penrose's chief political lieutenants, refused to accept Mellon as the boss. The Manufacturers' Association, interested primarily in high tariffs in the national field and in the passage of favorable legislation and the suppression of visionary (and costly) welfare and labor laws on the state level, did not entirely trust the financial interests represented by Mellon. Moreover, the manufacturers were accustomed, by long usage, to having their wishes respected at the state capitol. Mellon, the financier and stock manipulator, was a disturbing factor in state politics.

So, for the next five years the control of the Republican Party in the Keystone State became the prize in a battle of financial giants. Both the Mellon and Grundy factions had tremendous campaign funds for the primary fights in which the issue was determined. Money gushed in a rich stream into every precinct on primary day. The general elections in November didn't matter. The Democrats were too few, and their organization too thoroughly dominated by the Republican machine, to matter. The Republican nominations for state office and for most local offices were equivalent to election.

In the 1922 primary the state organization, headed by Mellon, selected George E. Alter, attorney general in the outgoing administration of Governor William C. Sproul, as its candidate for the nomination for governor. Grundy supported Gifford Pinchot, who had been state forester in the Sproul administration and who had been a controversial figure in the sub-cabinet of President Taft. Pinchot's reputation as a political progressive was based entirely on his zeal for the conservation of natural resources and on his 1912 support of Theodore Roosevelt in the Bull Moose campaign. So far as the Pennsylvania manufacturers were concerned, Pinchot was "safe." The primary election resulted in a victory for Pinchot over Alter —and for Grundy over the Mellon leadership.

Governor Pinchot and Mellon were at odds during most of the succeeding four years, and little legislation of any sort came out of Harrisburg.

In 1926, Pinchot being ineligible for re-election, Grundy backed John S. Fisher, who had been banking commissioner under Sproul, while Mellon and the state organization supported Edward E. Beidleman, who had been lieutenant governor with Sproul. Again Grundy's candidate won, and the head of the Manufacturers' Association became the recognized boss of the state, with a firm grip on the state capitol at Harrisburg.

Out of the 1926 primary, in which Grundy established his state leadership, grew one of the nation's famous election scandals, the "purchase" of a seat in the United States Senate by Philadelphia boss William S. Vare.

The state organization had put up George Wharton Pepper for the senate nomination, while Grundy backed Governor Pinchot. With the state machine thus split, the Philadelphia boss, who had been a member of the House of Representatives for ten years, decided to promote himself to the Senate. He was successful in winning the nomination in a three-way race, and was duly elected in November.

Pennsylvania's high-priced primaries had become so notorious, however, that the Senate was forced to take notice of the charges that grew out of the Vare-Pepper-Pinchot primary. An investigation which followed showed not only excessive expenditures by all the candidates, but bribery, vote-buying and concealment of the sources of some contributions. Vare was denied his seat and, in 1929, Governor Fisher, whose own primary expenditures fortunately were not subject to Senate review, appointed Grundy, his sponsor and chief source of campaign funds, to fill the vacancy pending a special election in 1930.

Grundy became a candidate for election to the office in 1930, the only time that he ever offered himself as a candidate for public office. He failed dismally in the primary, being possibly somewhat handicapped by the spectre of another Senate investigation of campaign expenditures.

The man who defeated Grundy, and who has remained something of a thorn in the side of the state boss ever since, was James J. "Puddler Jim" Davis, a one-time iron and steel worker who had served as Secretary of Labor under Presidents Harding, Coolidge and Hoover. Davis is director general of the Loyal Order of Moose, a member of the Masons (thirty-third degree), Mystic Shrine, Grotto, Odd Fellows, Knights of Pythias, Elks, Eagles, Foresters, Protected Home Circle, Knights of the Golden Eagle, Woodmen of the World, Maccabees, and the Amalgamated Association of Iron, Steel and Tin Workers of America, as well as being an honorary member of Delta Sigma Phi, the Veterans of Foreign Wars and the Spanish War Veterans.

Through the 1920's, and until 1931, Philadelphia elections, as well as those for state office, bore a general resemblance to the one-party politics of Texas or Mississippi, with the party labels reversed. There would be a rip-snorting, name-calling primary campaign for the Republican nominations; and then the general election day would pass quietly and almost unnoticed. The Republican nominees were, in effect, automatically elected.

A Democratic organization existed in Philadelphia, but only as a tail to the Republican kite. The Quaker City Democratic leaders for many years had been Charles P. Donnelly and Thomas J. Ryan. In practice, they were collateral members of the Republican city organization, with a status about equal to that of minor ward leaders. That was true when Penrose and McNichol headed the Republican machine, and the situation remained unchanged when Vare took over as boss. The Democratic leaders took orders. In return, they were permitted to name the minority party members of various commissions and boards, and thus to maintain a small Democratic organization.

The first stirrings toward the formation of an effective Democratic organization in Philadelphia followed shortly after the entrance into the city's newspaper publishing field of J. David Stern, who had been cutting his teeth as a publisher-politician across the river in Camden, New Jersey.

Stern bought the *Philadelphia Record*, a moribund morning newspaper, from the estate of Rodman Wanamaker and proceeded to turn it into a vigorous and liberal competitor to M. L. Annenberg's *Philadelphia Inquirer*, which had long been known as "the Bible of the Republican Party in Pennsylvania." Stern arrived on the scene in 1928, just in time to start whooping it up for Democratic presidential candidate Alfred E. Smith. While Smith did not come close to carrying Philadelphia, he did receive a large vote and carried several wards. The *Record*, well launched as a crusading, liberal newspaper, became the rallying point, and Stern, one of the leaders of the political uprising that was induced by the depression after 1929.

Another Democratic leader was arising at the other end of the state, in Pittsburgh. As the time for the 1932 Democratic National Convention drew near, Joseph F. Guffy, an independent oil producer, who had been slumbering unnoticed in the post of Democratic National Committeeman from Pennsylvania ever since the Democrats were ousted from power in Washington in 1920, suddenly leaped into action.

Guffey had been director of the bureau of sales of the Alien Property Custodian's office after the World War and had been indicted by Harding's Attorney General, Harry Daugherty, for an alleged shortage in his accounts. The indictment was never pressed and was finally wiped off the books. Guffey charged that Daugherty attempted to use the indictment to persuade him to give the lowdown on some of the deals of A. Mitchell Palmer, Daugherty's predecessor in the Wilson administration.

As it later developed, Guffey also had failed, on the plea of poverty, to pay several hundred thousand dollars of federal income tax, although he had fully complied with the law by filing returns on all of his income. When this fact was brought out some years later, Guffey was a member of the United States Senate. The Scripps-Howard newspaper in Pittsburgh rode the issue for all it was worth. For a time, hundreds of Pittsburgh residents were writing to the Collector of Internal Revenue: "I'll pay my tax when Senator Guffey pays his."

In 1932, however, with no clear idea of what the future would bring, but with bright hopes that a Democratic victory would restore his shattered personal fortunes, National Committeeman Guffey was carefully considering which bandwagon he had better jump aboard. By a shrewd or fortunate guess he picked the right man. He tied himself firmly to the coattails of New York's Governor Franklin D. Roosevelt—an attachment that he has never since relinquished.

Democrats in Pennsylvania were almost as scarce in 1932 as Republicans in the Solid South, but the Keystone State's delegation to the National Convention was a prize worth fighting for. Most people expected that it would line up for Al Smith, but Guffey, by adroit maneuvering, placed it in the Roosevelt column. And he was one of the first to realize the political advantages of having been a "for Roosevelt before Chicago" man.

Roosevelt's nomination, and prospective election in November, had the same effect on the "Forgotten Man" in Pennsylvania that it had throughout the country, but the Republican machine was sufficiently well entrenched to hold back the tide for a brief moment. President Hoover carried the state, but by a greatly reduced majority. In Philadelphia, where Republican majorities in the '20s had run close to 300,000, the machine could deliver only a 70,000 majority against Roosevelt.

Allegheny County, including Pittsburgh, center of the steel producing and coal mining industries, went Democratic for the first time in modern history. The county Democratic leader, who was rewarded promptly with appointment as Internal Revenue Collector in Pittsburgh, was David L. Lawrence. He has since survived—with little damage to his reputation—a politically inspired indictment for vote frauds, blackmail and bribery, and is now State Chairman and National Committeeman. Under his leadership Pittsburgh has remained a Democratic stronghold throughout the Roosevelt era.

At the time that President Roosevelt's first election raised up a general rebellion against it, the Philadelphia machine was handicapped by the fact that Vare, a victim of a paralytic stroke in 1928, was still holding the reins of leadership, although he was neither physically nor mentally capable of a vigorous leadership.

The machine had ruled Philadelphia for a gene-

ration without any opposition party to discipline
it and since the death of Penrose in 1921 it had not
even had any strong opposition within the Republican Party. But despite all of these weakening
factors, the Vare machine, even after the ouster
and death of its leader in 1934, and despite a four-
year Democratic administration in the state, managed to hold on to its control in Philadelphia, with
only minor setbacks, throughout the political revolution that followed.

The success of the machine is based on rigid
discipline and loyalty; on liberal use of city funds
for patronage, in which nearly all of the active
workers share; on the lavish use of election day
campaign funds, which the machine never lacks,
and, traditionally, on vote frauds and strong-arm
methods, for which Philadelphia has been notorious in the past.

More than two years after President Roosevelt
took up his White House residence, a checkup
showed that forty-six of the fifty members of the
Republican City Committee had public jobs, with
salaries ranging up to $15,000 a year; most of them
in the $5,000 to $8,000 bracket. The City Committee, consisting of one member (usually the
ward leader) from each of the fifty wards, included two representatives in Congress, twelve city
councilmen, five magistrates, the sheriff, and as-
sorted court clerks, members of the state legisla-

ture, appraisers and assessors. Thus all were cared for.

At the same time, and despite the loss of the county offices the previous year, three-fifths of the 3,000 precinct committeemen were on the public payroll at salaries averaging $2,237 a year. The *Record* put the cost of Philadelphia's "Bureau of Bosses"—the Vare machine—at $8,000,000 a year in city salaries paid to ward leaders, Vare henchmen and hangers-on.

The precinct committeemen, known also as division leaders (a division is a precinct), are the doorbell-ringers and stair-climbers, the men who are directly responsible for getting out the machine vote on election or primary day. The division leader is expected to know every voter in his district and to have as many of them as possible under direct obligation to him for favors. Political favors, the "fixing" of minor law violations, reduction of assessments, and the other normal and routine services of a political machine to its constituents, are rigidly routed through channels, in order to draw the utmost effectiveness from them, and also as a means of enforcing discipline within the machine itself. The division leader who is not in good standing with his ward leader cannot "deliver" to his constituents and quickly loses his power, and his job.

Political sinews of war have always been strengthened in Philadelphia by a direct assessment on the salaries of all public employes whose jobs are subject to the control of the machine. On the day before election the Republican City Committee meets and the ward leaders get their election orders and campaign funds. Allowances for campaign expenses may vary from $50 to $150 or more for each of the city's approximately 1,400 precincts. The money is handed out to each ward leader in an amount governed by the size of his ward and the number and importance of the contests to be decided. Under the Pennsylvania election laws, poll watchers may be paid $10 for the day, and four or five such watchers may be hired by each party, depending on the state of its exchequer, in each precinct. The jobs as watchers go to men in each division who, because of large family connections, or for any other reason, can "control" from ten to thirty or forty votes each.

"Hampy" Moore, who as mayor had thrown in his lot with the Vares after the death of Penrose in 1921, was back in City Hall when the New Deal storm struck in 1932. Moore had been elected by the machine a year earlier, and was safe for another three years. But under the system of divided city elections, the choice of important "row" officers—controller, receiver of taxes, treasurer and county officials—was due in 1933.

The Democrats, for the first time in a genera-

tion, prepared to put up a real battle. They drew
strength and inspiration from the name of President Roosevelt, who had captured the country's
imagination with his "hundred days'" blitzkrieg
against the depression. Postmaster General Farley
helped by the judicious use of federal patronage.
Locally, the party revival was sparked by "Dave"
Stern and the revitalized *Record*.

John O'Donnell, who had succeeded to the
Democratic city chairmanship, was as much a part
of the Vare organization as his predecessors, Donnelly and Ryan, had been. There was nothing to be
hoped for from him. Stern persuaded John B.
Kelly, handsome former Olympic rowing champion and a wealthy contractor, to assume the leadership of the Independent Democratic Committee,
a new party organization. The Stern-Kelly group
carried the September primary, nominating its candidates over those proposed by O'Donnell, and
then went on gathering strength as the November
election approached.

Anti-Vare Republicans, headed by Harry A.
Mackey, a former mayor who had tried to take
over Vare's leadership in an unsuccessful revolt in
1929, organized to support the Democratic candidates under the title of the Town Meeting Party.
They were actively aided by Governor Pinchot,
who provided state patronage for the anti-Vare
group.

Officially reported expenditures by the Vare machine amounted to $106,000 in the 1933 campaign. Whatever the actual expenditures amounted to, the sum was not enough to win. The opposition acknowledged the expenditure of $61,000, of which $30,000 was raised and spent by the anti-Vare Republican group. This latter group accounted for only 35,000 votes on election day—or at the rate of about $1 a vote.

The effective election day organization of the anti-machine forces threw the Vare organization off its stride. Democratic watchers were on duty everywhere. Observers reported that there was less fraud and strong-arm work at the polls than there had been at any previous Philadelphia election in many years.

The Democratic-Fusion victory in 1933 was complete, but the Penrose charter of 1919 saved the machine from disaster. It lost control temporarily of one-third of the city administration, but the mayoralty and the judicial offices, with their extensive patronage, were not at stake. They remained in the hands of the machine, providing strength for a later comeback to full dominance of the city government.

Within a few months after the 1933 defeat, the ill and discredited Vare was ousted as leader of the Philadelphia machine in a party revolt parallel to that which at the same time ousted John F. Curry as leader of Tammany Hall in New York City following the 1933 election of Mayor LaGuardia. Vare died two months later.

Vare's overthrow coincided with the rise of a new Republican power in Philadelphia: Joseph N. Pew, Jr., a member of the multi-millionaire family that controls the Sun Oil Company and the Sun Shipbuilding Company.

Pew, as a political leader, is almost as much a creation of President Roosevelt as is "Joe" Guffey. Prior to Roosevelt's election in 1932, the Sun Oil magnate had seldom taken any part in state or national politics, beyond the usual annual campaign contribution. But once Roosevelt got into the White House, Pew began a personal crusade to put a political end to Roosevelt and his New Deal.

Pew's method of acquiring political power was simple, direct and effective. He simply opened his purse to any worthy Republican candidate or campaign. It is conservatively estimated that up to the beginning of 1944 his fight against President Roosevelt had cost Pew more than $1,000,000. He boasted that if it finally took every penny of his fortune to remove Roosevelt from the White House he would consider the money well spent.

Early in the New Deal days, Pew took a trip to Washington to see what the Republican National Committee was doing to stop Roosevelt from winning a second term. He was amazed to find

GOP headquarters deserted except for a telephone operator and a clerk-caretaker. Pew indignantly sought out the national GOP leaders and demanded that a functioning headquarters be set up and equipped with an expert publicity staff. The party bigwags, recognizing a sucker, said that would take money. Pew said he would pay the bills. He did, but nothing that Pew could do could stem the New Deal flood, even in his home state.

Guffey, the F.R.B.C. man, had been hard at work in his home city of Pittsburgh. "Dave" Lawrence, given some Democratic sentiment to work with, was proving an effective machine builder. The once potent Republican organization in the steel city, formerly headed by William Flinn, who made a fortune of $11,000,000, mostly out of public works contracts, had been completely toppled. And Guffey had been busy, too, building up a party organization among the strongly pro-Roosevelt miners in the coal fields and among the steel workers.

In 1934 Guffey, with the aid of Lawrence and Philadelphia publisher Stern, put together a state ticket headed by George H. Earle, Jr., a heavy Democratic campaign contributor and F.D.R.'s Minister to Australia, and as the candidate for lieutenant governor, Thomas Kennedy of Lewis' United Mine Workers. For himself Guffey took the nomination for United States Senator. In

November the revitalized Philadelphia and Pittsburgh organizations, with the aid of the mining
and steel counties, swept the whole Democratic
ticket into office.

The impossible had happened in Pennsylvania.
Lawrence became Secretary of the Common-
wealth, Number One political adviser of the Earle
administration, and state chairman.

The "forgotten man" in Philadelphia was ready,
by then, to vote for President Roosevelt or for
anybody carrying Roosevelt's colors in any state
or national contest. But when it came down to
a matter of municipal government, where the jobs
of many thousands of members and beneficiaries
of the machine depended on the continued dominance of the Vare organization, the shoe was on
the other foot. The Republican machine, well
oiled with Pew's money, could still deliver a slim
majority for S. Davis Wilson, the machine's candidate for mayor, in 1935.

"Joe" Pew hoped that the Roosevelt madness
had begun to run out. With a naïvete that few of
the more experienced party leaders shared, he fore-
saw the defeat of the President and the election of
Alf M. Landon in 1936. Pew opened his purse
wider in the hope of clinching the victory.

But Philadelphia was "safe" only for local candidates. The machine's complete inability to cope
with the much bigger vote that was brought out

by a presidential contest, or even to control the presidential choices of many of its own members, was proved when President Roosevelt swept the city by 210,000 plurality, a figure rivaling the lop-sided Republican majorities of the 1920's.

The President carried Pittsburgh by 190,000—running better than two-to-one in that city—and swept Pennsylvania into the Democratic column by a total plurality of 664,000 votes over hapless Landon. He carried 40 of the 67 counties—in a state that had had no Democratic party worthy of the name six years earlier, and that had been ac-customed to Republican majorities of over a million votes.

The United Mine Workers and the CIO had been incorporated into the Guffey-run state ma-chine and their members were almost 100 per cent for the Democratic candidates. A CIO-UMW man was lieutenant governor of the state. The WPA vote had been organized. Dave Lawrence's machine had tipped Pittsburgh definitely into the Demo-cratic column. In Philadelphia the new Jack Kelly Democratic organization was able to put up a real battle for the Vareville vote. Alert Democratic watchers were at the polls and the elections could no longer be stolen. Some able political students believed that the Democrats were likely to control the state government for the next twenty years.

The prompt collapse of this prospect was due to

nothing Pew or Grundy could do, but entirely to a wide open split in the newly welded Democratic machine. Both Guffey and Lawrence had ambitions to succeed Earle as governor. President Roosevelt's services were enlisted as a mediator and he suggested William C. Bullitt, then Ambassador to France, as a compromise candidate. Philadelphia's Jack Kelly and Matthew H. McCloskey, a wealthy contractor whom Kelly had drawn into the Philadelphia picture as Democratic co-leader, opposed Bullitt. Lawrence cast in his lot with them, and so did Governor Earle.

As a result, the State Committee, dominated by Earle and Lawrence, endorsed Charles A. Jones, a Pittsburgh lawyer of no political prominence, as the candidate for governor. Guffey, Stern and the CIO got behind laborite Lieutenant Governor Thomas Kennedy for the gubernatorial nomination.

Meanwhile, Democratic Attorney General Charles J. Margiotti had brought a series of graft charges against Governor Earle and David Lawrence. The politically starved Democrats in the state administration, it appeared, had tried to cash in too quickly—and too crudely—on their control over state contracts.

The governor fought back spiritedly, using his power as chief executive to oust Margiotti from office, and calling the legislature into session—in

Huey Long fashion—to suspend a Dauphin County grand jury investigation of state affairs.

The primary fight in May, 1938, between Jones and Kennedy, with Margiotti entering the lists as a hopeless third candidate, measured up fully to the Democratic tradition of destructive internal fights. The respective candidates plastered each other thoroughly with mud. The Earle-Lawrence combination triumphed, nominating Jones for governor and Earle for United States Senator, but by the time the primary campaign was over, neither nomination was worth having. The courts meanwhile had upheld the Margiotti grand jury investigation and during the campaign Lawrence was indicted for blackmail, conspiracy and election law violations and 76 of Governor Earle's political allies and subordinates were indicted for fraud on highway contracts.

The Democratic primary victors were thoroughly discredited in the public eye. The CIO vote was estranged by defeat of Kennedy for the nomination for governor.

In the November election the Republican nominee for governor, Arthur H. James, a dull, colorless candidate, heavily financed by the Pew-Grundy machine, recaptured Pennsylvania for the GOP. James carried Philadelphia by only 10,000 plurality and lost Pittsburgh by 31,000, but the vote outside the two big cities rolled his state-wide plurality up to 279,000, a meager majority for the state of Quay and Penrose, but quite sufficient for all practical purposes.

Governor Earle, as candidate for United States Senator, was even more thoroughly trounced by Senator "Puddler Jim" Davis, who had again upset the Old Guard machine by winning renomination on the Republican ticket.

Grundy, unable to beat Davis himself, had put up as the machine candidate for the senatorial nomination G. Mason Owlett, who was counsel for the Pennsylvania Manufacturers' Association and the manager of one of Grundy's own enterprises, the Pennsylvania Manufacturers' Casualty Association. But the Keystone State Republicans were no more ready to vote for Grundy's business associate than they were for Grundy himself. "Puddler Jim," the Moose, Mason, Odd Fellow, Knight of Pythias, Golden Eagle, Woodman, Elk, Eagle, Forester, Protector of the Home Circle, Mystic Shriner, Maccabeean and Iron, Steel and Tin Worker of America, was renominated by a two-to-one vote. He remained a serious nuisance to the orderly rule of the machine, although hardly a menace to Pennsylvania's big business interests.

The recapture of Harrisburg by the Republicans came just in the nick of time to save the Philadelphia machine from possible disaster. With the help of a friendly state administration the machine, in the Fall of 1939, held on to the Philadelphia City Hall, but only by the slim margin of 30,000 votes in a total of 750,000. The vote was 390,335 for Republican candidate Robert E. Lambertson, and 360,679 for his Democratic opponent, Robert C. White.

Just a year later, Roosevelt again swept Philadelphia by 177,000 plurality over Wendell L. Willkie, while carrying Pittsburgh and Allegheny County by 105,000. The state, apart from its two big cities, gave a plurality for Willkie. But the Roosevelt vote in Philadelphia and Pittsburgh was sufficient to give him the state by 281,000 plurality, and to carry "Joe" Guffey back into office for a second six-year term as United States Senator.

Throughout the whole Roosevelt era, there had been one remarkable thing about the Philadelphia vote, which must be set down as a tribute to the efficacy of the Penrose-Vare-Pew-Grundy machine. The number of Republican votes has been almost constant in all of the elections, regardless of the personality of the candidates or the offices for which they were running, and despite the wide range in the total size of the vote.

The Republican vote was 329,881 for President in 1936; 417,050 for governor in 1938 (when at least 50,000 Democrats voted GOP because of the Earle administration scandals and the party split); 390,355 for mayor in 1939; 354,878 for President,

353,237 for United States Senator and 353,983 for state auditor in 1940; and from 311,000 to 316,000 for county and judicial officers in light off-year voting in 1941.

During these years the total vote varied from 887,000 to 625,000, and the Democratic totals went up and down in a correspondingly wide range. The Democrats polled a rock-bottom of about 310,000 for local candidates in the off-year 1941 municipal elections, and as high as 540,000 in the presidential years, when some 200,000 independents voted.

In both parties the amount of straight-party voting has been remarkably high. Four county officers, seven judges and eight magistrates were elected in 1941. The elections were close, with the Republican candidates across the board getting from 311,000 to 316,000 votes. Democratic candidates received 307,000 to 309,000 in almost every instance. The incumbent Democratic controller, Robert C. White, received 312,882 votes and was re-elected by a margin of 1,600.

"Joe" Pew can hardly be said to have distinguished himself for anything but ineptness and failure so far in the field of national politics. But he has never stopped trying.

After the 1936 debacle, Pew attached Landon's campaign manager and National Chairman, John D. M. Hamilton, to his personal political staff, putting him in as a member of the Philadelphia law firm headed by George Wharton Pepper, Pew's personal counsel. That association has continued, with Hamilton as Pew's chief adviser on campaign strategy in the national field.

Pew favored Senator Robert A. Taft for the Republican presidential nomination in 1940, but readily agreed to the plan to have the Pennsylvania delegation vote, at the start, for Governor James as a "favorite son" candidate, until it could be seen which way the wind was likely to blow.

The Taft managers waited patiently for Pew to throw the delegation to the Ohio senator on one of the early ballots. But the Pew strategy was bankrupt and its leadership was indecisive. Forlornly the Pennsylvania delegation stuck to Governor James. It was in caucus when Wendell L. Willkie was being nominated.

During the crucial hours just before the nomination of Willkie, Pew was in his Main Line home taking a bath, with his Oriental butler under strict orders that he was not to be disturbed.

There was no love lost between Pew and Willkie in the campaign. In a pre-convention interview with a reporter for the Philadelphia *Evening Bulletin*, Willkie bluntly stated: "I don't like Joe Pew's brand of politics."

But Pew's intense opposition to President Roosevelt made him go the limit in Willkie's behalf.

Toward the close of the campaign, when Willkie was touring Michigan after his Western trip, Pew sent Hamilton to join the Willkie train and take over the political management of the campaign. Hamilton was coldly received, and left the party at Grand Rapids, after a one-day stay.

While Pew has been markedly unsuccessful in national politics, he and "Joe" Grundy have done very well on their home grounds. Their state machine copper-riveted its grip on Philadelphia and on the state capitol at Harrisburg with the election of Major General Edward Martin as governor in 1942 and of Bernard Samuel as mayor in 1943.

It cost the Pew-Grundy machine an estimated $1,500,000 to win the nomination for General Martin in a hot primary contest in which their control of the state organization again was challenged by Senator Davis.

The state bosses knew better than to take lightly the threat of "Puddler Jim." When he became a candidate for the nomination for governor, the Pew-Grundy combine sent emissaries to him in Washington with offers of a peaceful settlement, in which he would have been cut in on the state leadership. But Davis was confident that he could lick the machine again and refused even to talk about withdrawing from the race. So the state political machine opened up with its big guns.

An old story of the indictment of Davis for conducting a lottery in connection with promotional activities for the Moose was dug up and broadcast to the state. Davis was charged with being in league with labor racketeers, and with having a secret understanding with John L. Lewis, under which the United Mine Workers' president would have been permitted to make appointments to state offices.

Davis hit back directly at the machine leaders. He asserted that General Martin had been a bankrupt during the depression and had paid off his debts at a few cents on the dollar. And, said Davis, if Martin were elected he would be dominated body and soul by Pew and Grundy and the big financial interests allied with them.

The Democrats later made the same charge—that Martin was completely controlled by reactionary big business—but it did them no good. Pew and Grundy nominated their man, and elected him with the aid of big GOP pluralities throughout most of the state outside Pittsburgh and Philadelphia. Martin carried Philadelphia by only 157 votes, which indicated, the opposition said, that the Democrats probably had polled an uncounted plurality of 10,000 to 15,000 votes.

Throughout the Roosevelt era, the Republican machine has held on to the city government, with the Democrats merely nibbling off bits of county and judicial patronage now and then. By 1943 the machine had won back virtually all of the offices that had been lost temporarily. It controlled 20 of the 22 councilmen.

The place of William S. Vare has never really been filled. Pew remains as the titular leader of the Philadelphia organization, but he lacks the training, ability and inclination to be the active head of a big-city political machine. Little leaders tend the actual mechanism of the organization and are inclined to regard Pew as a "fat cat," whose money they are glad to accept, but whose views on political strategy they distrust. Two judges are regarded as the strongest factors in keeping the machine together. They are Charles L. Brown, chief judge of the municipal court, which has a patronage payroll of $1,000,000 a year, and Harry S. McDevitt, president judge of the Common Pleas Court, No. 1. Each of them has had a lifetime of training in the machine, and each exerts a wide influence over groups of ward leaders.

Bernard Samuel, who was elected mayor in 1943, defeating former ambassador Bullitt, is the tool of the machine, rather than its boss.

A South Philadelphia ward leader of no outstanding ability, Mayor Samuel served for years in the city council, never once deviating from the line laid down by the machine. While in the council he worked as a board room clerk in a brokerage house, a position roughly equivalent to that of an office boy. His duties consisted of chalking up prices on the stock board. When seniority made him chairman of the finance committee of the council, his brokerage house promoted him to the job of head of the board room, making him, in effect, the head office boy.

Grundy, in his eighty-second year, remains the dominant figure in the party, both in Philadelphia and in the state organization. Grundy sits on his money bags and makes the leaders come to him, and he gets what he wants. Pew and Grundy are a team. Pew's main ambition is to rid the country of Roosevelt—an objective which Grundy approves. Grundy's chief interest is to see that his fellow manufacturers are protected—a purpose to which Pew has no objections.

Guffey is the nominal leader of the Democratic Party, but his power depends on strategy and persuasion. He cannot dictate to "Dave" Lawrence, the Pittsburgh leader, or to James P. Clark, owner of a large and profitable trucking business, who succeeded "Jack" Kelly as Philadelphia city chairman.

The Democratic Party in Pennsylvania remains a Roosevelt party, with its strength centered in Pittsburgh, Philadelphia and the coal and steel areas. No single man, and no three or four men, can boss it except as they attach themselves to the

Roosevelt program and so put themselves at the head of the Roosevelt forces in the state. That is the secret of Guffey's continued success; he has never cut loose for a moment from the President as the individual leader of the Democratic Party, nor from the program advocated by the President.

7

MAILED FIST IN TENNESSEE

FROM THE benevolent dictatorship of Boss Ed
Crump in Memphis, to the gunman-terrorized
domain of Sheriff Birch Biggs in rural Polk County,
300 miles to the east, Tennessee has the unenviable
distinction of being America's most bossed state in
1944.

Crump in his old age is still the absolute, arbitrary, and almost undisputed ruler of Memphis,
with its quarter of a million population, and of
Shelby County, in which reside 100,000 persons
outside the city of Memphis. The 50,000 to 60,000
Shelby County pluralities, which the Crump machine can deliver when pushed, give the boss an
unbeatable balance of power in naming United
States senators, governors, and all other public
officials elected by a state-wide vote. Not one state
official has been elected in more than a decade
without Crump's support.

The Memphis boss rules with amazing cynicism. He openly makes and breaks governors as well as mayors. He takes delight in making public officials acknowledge publicly their obligation and loyalty to him. Any show of independence is likely to result in the offender being driven forever from public life. If the offense occurs in Memphis, the culprit may be driven out of business and, literally, out of the city.

Way across the state there has developed during the past twenty years, and particularly in the past ten years, a machine of equal potency, although of smaller dimensions. Sheriff Biggs' Polk County organization is that anomaly of American politics —a rural Tammany Hall. Since 1938 it has reached out tentacles into at least four adjoining agricultural counties. Its reign of terrorism and intimidation has drawn the unfavorable attention of the United States Department of Justice on more than one occasion. Underlings of Sheriff Biggs have been convicted of offenses against free elections. The United States Supreme Court has taken notice of the sheriff's own complicity in the overriding of civil rights in his county. But Sheriff Biggs is not a man to be deflected from his purposes by mere judicial slaps on the wrist. He still runs his own county as an absolute despotism and, with frank mountaineer humor, he has begun to talk about his outlying territories as "occupied countries."

But in the Tennessee story, Boss Crump comes first.

II

Edward Hull Crump, now sixty-eight, moved to Memphis from Mississippi at the age of seventeen. He started out as a bookkeeper and credit man, but soon went into business for himself as a saddlery goods dealer. Meanwhile, he became active in ward politics. By careful political spadework and plenty of personal color, he rose rapidly to the top of the heap. Within ten years after he arrived in Memphis Ed Crump had established himself as the Democratic boss, a position that he has held, and increasingly fortified, during the succeeding forty years.

Crump has run for office twenty-two times and has never been defeated. He has been mayor four times, county trustee four times and Representative in Congress twice. His last campaign was in 1939, when he was elected as mayor and served one minute.

The Memphis-Shelby County machine has all the usual ingredients, plus some. Crump has complete power over every city, county, state and federal employe in Shelby County. The fact that Memphis has a municipally owned and operated light, gas and water system, gives the political machine a larger-than-average patronage payroll.

In addition to controlling the big vote represented by the public employes and their families, Crump attracts the support of the average voter by his claim of efficient government, and the subaverage voters by showmanship. Business men are kept in line by not too subtle threats, and examples, of intimidation.

Memphis actually is a well run town, if you like dictatorships. The police force is highly efficient, tax rates are low, and there have been no notable graft scandals in recent city history. Some years ago Police Commissioner Joe Boyle received a mandate to clean out gambling and vice, and within a surprisingly short time gambling houses and redlight districts were virtually extinct in Memphis.

There is nothing illusory about Crump's ability to deliver the vote of Shelby County either in the general election or in the primary. When Gordon Browning was nominated for governor in 1936 with Crump's endorsement, Shelby County gave him 59,874 votes against 878 for two opponents, one of whom had the endorsement of United States Senator Kenneth McKellar. Browning broke with Crump during his term, as most governors prior to Prentice Cooper, the three-term incumbent, have done. When Browning sought renomination in 1938, in the bitterest of modern day Tennessee election fights, Shelby County gave him 9,315 votes and Cooper, the Crump-backed candidate, got 57,255.

But, powerful in vote-getting as he is, Crump does not depend too much on the voice of the people. Shelby County returns are traditionally the last to come in during a state election and, however large a lead a Crump opponent may have coming into Shelby County, the Crump majority there is always larger. With the rest of the state even moderately split, Crump's 60,000 votes in Shelby can decide any state election. After the 1942 election the Memphis *Press-Scimitar*, which offers the only consistent opposition to the machine within Shelby County, obtained affidavits from many voters indicating clearly that candidates opposed by the machine did not get a fair count. Election-night counts from individual polling places, as gathered by newspaper reporters from the election officials on the spot, were mysteriously changed when the official count was announced. But since there is no semblance of open organized opposition in Memphis, such evidences of fraud are never effectively capitalized.

Many of the details of the Crump organizational methods always have been carefully guarded. He is said to have a card index which lists every voter in Shelby County. He is also understood to have taught Huey Long a good deal about the details of running a political machine.

Crump regards with open and complete cynicism the question of the Negro vote. Early in his career he found the Negro vote of value. In one campaign he had his workers travel up and down Beale Street with huge blackboards, teaching Negroes to spell the name of his write-in candidate. Crump's man won, with strong Negro support, and the story is told that to this day many Memphis Negroes can spell nothing but that candidate's name.

Crump controlled the Negro vote through a Negro lieutenant. But when his agent grew restless and began to show signs of independence, Crump threw a police line in front of the man's business establishment, had every person entering it searched, and so effectively wrecked the man's business that he gave up and moved to Chicago. The boss' ruthlessness in that case is typical of his manner in dealing with anyone, inside the machine or out, who opposes him. Watkins Overton was mayor and right-hand man to Crump for twelve years. During the negotiations for the city purchase of the water and light system, Overton disagreed with the boss over some matter which was never disclosed, but which was believed to be trivial. Crump, in ditching the mayor in the next, 1939, election, simply announced that Overton "wouldn't follow along with us, so like everybody else who won't stick with the organization on all matters, we kicked him out."

A bright youth in the Crump machine, C. C. Brown, a member of the boss' delegation in the state legislature, offended Crump at one of the latter's annual parties for the organization. The usual version is that Crump called Brown from a bridge game to play in a ball game and later learned that Brown had grumbled about having to leave the bridge table. Crump was furious. Brown, frightened, issued a public statement apologizing for anything he might have done to offend the boss. But it wasn't enough. Brown's name, already on the official list of organization candidates for re-election, was withdrawn. Brown attempted to practice law in Memphis for a year or two, then gave up and moved to Nashville.

County Clerk Gerald Stratton had served the machine faithfully for years and had been re-elected regularly as an efficient and competent public official. Several years ago he wrote Crump a letter saying that he was no longer in sympathy with the organization's methods. Crump was not satisfied with defeating Stratton overwhelmingly at the next election; he started one bitter personal attack after another against him, charging that Stratton never had been any good. Stratton moved out of the state.

Crump, at the same time, has rewarded those who faithfully and unquestioningly followed his orders. He trained Clifford Davis step by step in the organization, made him city judge and city commissioner in Memphis, and, finally, sent him to Congress. Similarly he advanced the colorless Walter Chandler in the same way, sending him to Congress and finally bringing him home to become mayor. He made a federal judge out of Marion Boyd, one of his machine lieutenants, and a collector of internal revenue out of Abe Waldaeur, another aide in running the machine.

The chief requirement for his assistants is that they must completely acquiesce in whatever the boss does. In his later years Boss Crump has taken a personal delight in forcing his creatures to humiliate themselves in public. Talking to a reporter in his office recently, Crump got a notion. Picking up a telephone, he called Mayor Chandler at City Hall. "Walter," he said, "I bet you don't know the words to 'America.'" A pause. "You do, huh? Well, let's hear you sing it." So the affairs of Memphis stood still while the mayor sang a song to Ed Crump. Governor Prentice Cooper finds it necessary to call Memphis or to confer with Crump's representatives at the state capitol before expressing himself on matters of even the slightest importance. Cooper has never shown any independence during his three terms; a whole series of governors before him had tried to assert themselves and had invariably, as in the case of Browning, been defeated for renomination. There is very little camouflage or dissembling of this state of affairs. The "boys" are frank about their leader. Probate Judge Sam Bates said in a 1942 speech for the machine slate: "Mr. Crump is the issue. No other community has ever had a political boss like Mr. Crump."

Crump even takes delight in displaying the subservience of the whole electorate.

When he decided in 1939 that Mayor Overton must be kicked out, it was late in the political season. The deadline for filing nominating petitions was approaching and no organization candidate had been decided upon. So the boss simply had a qualifying petition circulated with the space for the candidate's name left blank. When plenty of signatures had been obtained, Crump suddenly decided to put his own name in the blank space. He was elected without opposition, was sworn in, resigned, and had the city commission name Walter Chandler as mayor. Crump explained that he had wanted Chandler to stay in Congress during the campaign period to support the Roosevelt administration's bill repealing the Neutrality Act.

Crump's one act as mayor was typical of his attitude toward minority groups. It was to announce that Memphis wanted none of the CIO convention, which was being considered for the

Tennessee city. But two years later, when the CIO, despite open and violent opposition by Crump's police, had organized sufficiently in Memphis to become a voting power, Crump sent Chandler to greet a CIO meeting in Memphis with the assurance that anything the boys wanted was theirs.

Crump has long been a supporter of the poll tax, which is an obvious aid to Southern political machines because it limits the size of the electorate which the machine is seeking to control. But some years ago Crump found a wave of opposition to the poll tax growing within the state, and announced that he favored its repeal. In Governor Prentice Cooper's campaigns in 1938 and 1940 one of the planks in his platform was state action to repeal the vote tax in Tennessee; but each time, after the election, repeal measures were killed by administration forces in the legislature. Cooper's promises in his 1942 campaign were more specific. This time the repeal bill passed—only to be declared unconstitutional by the State Supreme Court, a majority of whose members owed their election entirely to Crump.

United States Senator Kenneth McKellar, the irascible and patronage-grabbing acting chairman of the Senate Appropriations Committee, has built up his own separate organization in the state outside Shelby County, but it acts as a unit with the Crump machine and is, in effect, an extension of

Crump's Shelby County organization. McKellar, almost as much as Tennessee's junior senator, Tom Stewart, wears his toga at the will of Boss Crump. The only time McKellar has tested his strength against the Crump machine, in the 1936 governorship primary, he was soundly beaten.

Boss Crump has supported President Roosevelt more consistently than Senator McKellar has, although he has not by any means been uniformly for the President. One of the most amusing incidents in the Senate fight against confirmation of former Democratic National Chairman Edward J. Flynn as Minister to Australia was the issuance by Crump of a public statement attacking Flynn as a "waterfront ward politician." McKellar, of course, joined the boss and was prepared to vote against confirming the appointment when Flynn decided to avoid the issue by having his name withdrawn.

Late in 1943 Crump jumped on the Roosevelt fourth term bandwagon when he issued a statement, phrased in typical Crump language:

"There is no justification for the 'solid South' bolting. The South has fared better than ever before. President Roosevelt will be the Democratic nominee if he wants it and he can choose his own Vice President. . . . There are three great dates—birth of Jesus Christ, birth of our Republic, and the years of Roosevelt's work since Pearl Harbor for the American people and the whole world."

Crump has a gift of colorful speech which seems to arise spontaneously, and which has been an asset to him in his political career. When former Representative Ridley Mitchell, running against Governor Cooper in the 1942 Democratic primary, sought support on the grounds that he had had a good record as a congressman some years back, Crump replied that even a buzzard is pure white until he is half grown. Objecting once to a newspaper account of one of his pronouncements, Crump told a reporter that the condensation of his statement was "as thin as a worn-out suit on a last year's humming bird."

Crump has become wealthy through his real estate and insurance business and investments. Other insurance companies find it hard sledding in his territory. Compulsion presumably is seldom necessary, but there have been cases in which heavy insurers—one specific instance being that of the operator of a tourist camp—have dropped policies in other companies with the statement that they had found that they could not do business unless they shifted to Crump's agency.

There are many evidences that this is the twilight of the rule of bosses, but Memphas has seen no evidence of any such tendency. Crump's power is as absolute and, apparently, as secure as ever. And his machine is solidly built. Whether it will outlast him remains to be seen.

III

Sheriff Birch Biggs, the Democratic boss of a sizeable section of rural east Tennessee, is a bluff, hearty, loud-mouthed, rough-and-tumble country-man whose distinguishing accoutrements are a ten-gallon hat and a free-swinging revolver.

For twenty years he and his son, Broughton Biggs, now a state senator, have alternately held the office of sheriff of Polk County. During that period they have built up a political machine which can deliver the Polk County vote almost solidly. By means of that absolute control, coupled with his influence in adjoining counties, Sheriff Biggs is able to dominate the election of the state senator in a district consisting of four counties and to in-fluence greatly the choice of the representative from the Third Congressional district, which em-braces twelve counties and includes the city of Chattanooga. United States Senators McKellar and Stewart woo the favor of the country boss; Ed Crump is not above seeking his help in a tight state primary contest.

Birch Biggs uses all the known instruments of political power. He controls what local political patronage there is. He maintains excellent and mu-tually advantageous relations with the Tennessee Copper Company, the only "big industry" in his immediate domain. And he is in a position to extend normal political favors through the local courts.

But, in what is normally a peaceful, civilized community of farms and small towns, Sheriff Biggs rules principally by means of terrorism and intimidation, backed by the pistol and the black-jack.

A paragraph of historical background will provide the stage setting.

The hill country of east Tennessee did not join the secession movement in 1861. It remained loyal to the Union and provided 30,000 volunteers for the Union army during the Civil War. It has always been Republican since then. The First and Second Congressional districts, in the Tennessee salient which juts out between North Carolina and Virginia, have been Republican steadily since 1858. On the fringe of this section, in the southeast corner of the state, lies Polk County, something of a "border" county, politically. It was normally Republican by up to 1,000 plurality before the rise of the Biggs machine, but it is now as overwhelmingly Democratic, in election day returns, as is South Carolina—or Memphis.

Birch Biggs, in his own person, is the Democratic Party in Polk County.

In the 1942 Democratic primary for the nomination of a candidate for governor, he gave Governor Prentice Cooper (Boss Crump's candidate)

3,970 votes to 50 for his opponent, former Representative Ridley Mitchell. In the same primary he gave 3,899 votes to United States Senator Stewart, a Crump candidate for renomination, and only 122 to Stewart's two Democratic opponents.

In the general election of November 3, 1942, in what had been a Republican county not so many years earlier, Sheriff Biggs allowed just 86 votes for E. N. Frazier, the Republican candidate for governor. Governor Cooper, the Democratic candidate for re-election, got 3,560.

Over the years, Biggs had expanded his influence beyond the borders of Polk County, into adjoining Bradley County, without encountering much opposition and without attracting much attention. But about six years ago, when he began to branch out in the other direction, into McMinn and Monroe Counties, he ran into difficulty because of the fact that he was invading another Congressional district.

Representative John Jennings, Jr., a Republican, whose home is in Knoxville, and whose district includes McMinn and Monroe Counties, became alarmed, and with good reason, by Sheriff Biggs' activities. In a district that has been as consistently Republican as have Maine and Vermont, Jennings saw the GOP majority whittled down from 16,143 votes in 1938 to 9,611 in 1940, and to a mere 2,529 in 1942. So Jennings, screaming "fraud" in a loud and indignant voice, ran to the Department of Justice of the Democratic administration in Washington.

In one of the election precincts of McMinn County in the 1940 election the three precinct election officials, after slugging a citizen who insisted on casting his own vote, had decided to close up the polling place—perhaps to prevent further disorder. That was at ten o'clock in the morning, one hour after the polls had opened. As a result of this informal and early calling off of the election, some 400 registered voters in the precinct had been unable to vote.

Jennings pointed out to the Department of Justice that this wasn't right. Attorney General Francis Biddle decided, after due consideration, that it wasn't even legal. It took two years for the combined efforts of Jennings and a United States Attorney General to bring the three culprits to justice. And when they had duly been convicted Federal District Judge Leslie R. Darr, sitting in Chattanooga, fined them one cent each.

Judge Darr, who had been appointed by President Roosevelt on the recommendation of Senator McKellar, observed from the bench that he didn't think he should be too hard on the guilty election officials because they were only following "the practice" in that part of the state.

Representative Jennings exploded in a wrathful

attack on Judge Darr and Sheriff Biggs alike on the floor of the House.

"Sheriff Biggs," he said, "is the author of election outrages in this section of Tennessee. Through them he has absolutely abolished free elections in Polk County. Having subjugated Polk County, Biggs has moved into McMinn and Monroe Counties in my district. He has habitually sent armed deputy sheriffs from Polk County into McMinn and Monroe Counties to aid in terrorizing their citizens on election day."

"Birch Biggs and his satellites," Jennings went on, "refer to McMinn and Monroe Counties as 'occupied counties.' They are seeking to put them on the level on which Hitler has placed France, Belgium, Holland, Norway, Poland, Czechoslovakia, and the other conquered countries of Europe."

It was not the first time Sheriff Biggs had been likened to Hitler. The same comparison had been used by some of the defense attorneys for a group of labor union members who fell into the sheriff's hands in 1939. This incident became something of a cause celebre in union and court annals under the title, "U. S. v. Anderson et al." It is briefly recorded here to illustrate, on an easily comprehendible scale, the close connection between "big business" and a closely held political machine.

In 1939 a strike occurred at the Copperhill mines of the Tennessee Copper Company, the only big industry in Polk County. Sheriff Biggs, who can depend on the company's owners for sizeable campaign contributions, promptly placed himself at the head of an army of two hundred deputy sheriffs—whose salaries were paid by the company.

For several months this army of strikebreakers systematically created a reign of terror in Polk County. From temporary headquarters on the company's property Biggs directed his specially deputized company guards in searching strikers' homes, stopping and searching all cars that were out after dark, and generally terrorizing the strikers and their families.

The strikers grew steadily more bitter. Finally, two power lines feeding the copper plant were blown up. Working with two F.B.I. agents, Biggs supervised a round-up of eighty suspects. They were taken to a Y.M.C.A. building on the company's grounds and held there and questioned intermittently for periods as long as six days, in some cases, until a series of confessions was obtained.

The convictions based on those confessions were reversed by the United States Supreme Court on March 1, 1943, in a decision that struck a body blow at the use of third degree methods by law enforcement officers.

Meanwhile, the methods by which Biggs' machine obtained its election day majorities were being exposed to public light in some other court proceedings, based on the activities of the sheriff's political satellites in McMinn and Monroe Counties.

The chairman and secretary of the McMinn County Board of Election Commissioners resigned their offices in the Fall of 1942. The resignations came promptly after a legal action had been filed, seeking their removal for gross violations of their trust. Here were some of the sworn charges, which the two top county election officials did not permit to come to trial:

In the court house at Athens, county seat of McMinn County, the Democratic election officer and two Democratic judges, all officiating at the biennial county election on August 6, 1942, were armed, and other armed men, from out of the county, were around the polling place all day. Voters and the Republican election judge were prevented from witnessing the count of the vote. Athens, lying about halfway between Chattanooga and Knoxville, has a population of 6,000 persons. It is the seat of Tennessee Wesleyan Junior College and of Grant Memorial University.

At Etowah (pop. 4,000) Policeman Clyde Rogers was the officer of the election in one precinct and he and the two Democratic election judges were openly armed during the election. At another precinct the election officer was Jim Cantrell, brother of Paul Cantrell, the outgoing sheriff and candidate for justice of the peace. When the polls closed the ballot boxes from both polling places were taken to the Cantrell Banking Company Building, owned by the brothers, and all voters, including H. D. Rule, the opposing candidate for re-election as justice of the peace, were excluded during the count. (The Tennessee election law prohibits presence of armed men within ten feet of a polling place. It also provides that voters may remain and witness the counting of the vote.)

In all elections in McMinn County in 1938, 1940 and 1942 the ballots were printed on transparent tissue paper, so that both the printed names of the candidates and the voters' marks showed through. The election officers, as they took the folded ballots and deposited them in the ballot boxes, could see whether the individual had voted "according to promise or reward."

In the 1940 election more than 1,500 absentee ballots were counted in McMinn County, at least twenty times the normal number. In the 1942 election more than 1,200 absentee ballots were counted. They had been mailed in bundles to the county election commissioners from Knoxville and other nearby cities.

Those were just a few of the charges which prompted the resignation of the McMinn County election officials.

In Monroe County, another of Sheriff Biggs'

"occupied counties," Sheriff W. O. Brakebill resigned shortly after he had been re-elected in 1942.
The reason: he had been served in an action
brought by his opponent to have the election declared invalid because of numerous frauds.

On election day, according to sworn charges
supported by many affidavits, Sheriff Brakebill sat
in a room in the Madisonville school house, across
from another room in which a polling booth was
situated. Madisonville, the county seat, is a country
town of 1,000 population.

The sheriff, it was alleged, had a large sum of
money which he parceled out in $2 and $3 payments to scores of voters who dropped by his room
before going to the voting booth. Sheriff Brakebill
also had a pile of ballots, already marked with a
cross by his name, according to the same charges.
Here was the system, as explained in the court papers: The voter, taking his $2 or $3, was handed
one of the pre-marked Brakebill ballots at the same
time. When he went into the other room to vote
he was given a clean ballot by the election officials,
but he was expected to drop the pre-marked ballot
in the box and deliver the clean ballot back to the
sheriff's election-day headquarters, across the hall.

The real flavor of the Monroe County election,
however, was to be found down at the Madisonville court house, where there was another polling
place. On election duty at the court house was a

whole regiment of Brakebills, some probably armed.

Mrs. Beula Brakebill, who was not only the sheriff's wife, but also the coroner of Monroe County, was ensconced in the office of the county judge. She was plentifully supplied with money which she paid out to voters during the day, it was charged.

In the room where the election was held were Rankin Brakebill, the sheriff's brother, who served as the officer of the election, with a pistol sticking in his belt; Joe Brakebill, a relative, who was a candidate for the office of county road superinten-dent; and Joe's son, D. M. Brakebill, also armed and serving as an election judge.

Former Sheriff Hugh Webster, the immediate predecessor of Brakebill, was named in the removal suit as having purchased more than one hundred votes at $2 each. "The bastards wanted $3, but I wouldn't pay 'em but $2 a head," he was quoted as saying.

Deputy sheriffs, armed with pistols, were on duty at every precinct as election officers and judges. There were vote-buyers at every polling place. Voters for Brakebill's opponent claimed that they were intimidated and terrorized. At the court house precinct, ten more votes were counted than there were voters. At the school house pre-cinct votes outnumbered the voters on the poll list by fifty-eight. At another polling place, election officials ran off with the ballot box before the votes were counted.

As already noted, Sheriff Brakebill resigned a few weeks after he had been re-elected, without letting these charges come to trial. But Brakebill and the McMinn County election commissioners who resigned under similar circumstances are minor characters, and their mishaps are cited only to show the election day methods that since the rise of Sheriff Birch Biggs have come to be recognized as "the practice" in a section of east Tennessee.

As for Boss Biggs, he is still riding high. In the past three years he has used his influence in the state legislature, with the sanction and aid of the big boss, "Ed" Crump, to solidify still further his position in Polk County and in the adjoining counties.

During the 1941 session of the legislature Biggs succeeded in getting through a series of "ripper" bills, which legislated out of office a group of elected Republican officials in McMinn County. The bills became a burning issue throughout the state, not so much because of their content as because of the unorthodox methods Biggs had to pursue in getting them passed.

The Tennessee Senate has a strong tradition, compounded of home rule sentiment and "senatorial courtesy," which requires that no bills of purely local application be favorably considered unless they are sponsored by the senator from the district which they would affect. McMinn County was represented by Senator R. D. Lindsay, a Republican, who, naturally, was violently opposed to Sheriff Biggs' "ripper" program. But Biggs, in flagrant violation of the home rule tradition, had his bills introduced by a Democrat from the western part of the state. They were supported by Boss Crump, passed by the legislature, and signed by Governor Cooper.

In 1943 a similar series of bills affecting Bradley County was passed and signed. This time Biggs had no difficulty in complying fully with the Senate's customs, traditions and forms. The bills were sponsored by his son, State Senator Broughton Biggs, whose district included Bradley County.

Sheriff Biggs obtained full recognition as a power in state elections during the 1942 campaign, when Senator Stewart and Governor Cooper were up for renomination and re-election. There was no difficult about re-electing the governor, but Senator Stewart faced strong Democratic opposition, despite his backing by Boss Crump.

Two weeks before the 1942 Democratic primary, some able political students in the state thought that Stewart was sure to be defeated by his opponent, Ned Carmack. But at that point Senator McKellar came down from Washington and took charge. Leaving Shelby County in the efficient hands of Boss Crump, McKellar devoted himself exclusively to the situation in east Tennessee.

The general interpretation of what happened was that McKellar and Biggs worked out a deal with the Republican organizations in the eastern counties, particularly those in the First Congressional district, where Representative Carroll Reece is the recognized Republican boss. Under this arrangement the east Tennessee Republicans voted in droves in the Democratic primary for Stewart; in return the Republicans were relieved of election day worry about some of their county officials whom the Democrats otherwise might have beaten.

To signalize his arrival as a real boss, Sheriff Biggs gave a big barbecue for his followers after the 1942 election. It cost $1,000 and in everything but size it rivaled even Boss Crump's annual post-election parties.

8

LOUISIANA PURCHASE

H UEY PIERCE LONG, the dictator-to-be of Louisiana, was five years old, just beginning to absorb the prejudices of his native small town in the Bible belt of central Louisiana, when machine politics were born in sophisticated New Orleans.

While the future Kingfish was testing his strength back in the sweet potato country, the city ring, frankly modeled after the Tammany Hall of Tweed and Croker, was perfecting its grip on the election machinery and municipal government of the easy-going French Catholic metropolis at the mouth of the Mississippi River.

And when the time came for Huey's cyclonic rise to power as the first dictator of an American state, it was the New Orleans city machine which stood as the greatest obstacle in his path. Huey never succeeded in crushing the machine, although he did finally take it over intact.

When the Dictator's own state machine crumbled to pieces after his death the only thing that remained—under new management but otherwise not much changed—was the New Orleans city machine, still dominant in municipal politics as it had been for a generation before the Kingfish was heard of.

The story of machine politics in Louisiana is the story of how the "Old Regulars" fought Huey Long to a standstill, bowed to him only after he had become absolute dictator of the rest of the state; but outlasted him and, in Chinese fashion, finally absorbed their conquerors.

The Choctaw Club of New Orleans, named, like Tammany, for an Indian tribe, came into being in 1898, simultaneously with the adoption by Louisiana of new suffrage and election laws. These laws had the purpose and effect of perpetuating the Democratic Party in power and of excluding Negroes from the Democratic primaries. (The number of Negro voters fell from 129,760 in 1896 to 5,380 in 1900.)

The machine which the Choctaws proceeded to build always has been concerned solely with control of the party primaries. In Louisiana, since 1900, "election" has meant "Democratic primary election."

Martin Behrman, a former beer salesman with a squatty beer-barrel figure and a despondent black mustache, who spoke an excellent brand of "Dem-and-Dose" Brooklynese, was the boss of the machine from 1900 until his death in 1926. He was also mayor of New Orleans from 1904 until his death, with the exception of a single "reform" administration from 1920 to 1924. As a result of this long dual capacity the principle that the mayor always was the boss of the political machine became firmly established in New Orleans.

Behrman was a leader who had fought his way up from the bottom of the pile. That he never had time to polish his English was perhaps due to the fact that he was too busy polishing his city machine and his mastery of political strategy. The machine was built on ward lines, with a leader who became a local boss in each of the city's seventeen wards. The ward leaders were personally responsible to the big boss of the city organization. Under each ward leader were the fifteen to eighteen precinct captains, appointed by him and responsible to him for getting out the vote. And each of the precinct captains had his three or four "ward heeler" helpers.

The strength of this organization was indicated as much by its popular names as by its uniform success in municipal elections. The machine was known as "the Choctaws," "the Ring" or as "the

Regulars." During a serious split in the organization in the early 'twenties the Behrman faction came to be known as the "Old Regulars." The "New Regulars" eventually disappeared from the scene, but the name, "Old Regulars," stuck to the organization.

The same political antipathy that is found in up-state New York toward New York City and in down-state Illinois toward Chicago exists in the country parishes of Louisiana toward New Orleans. But whereas New York and Chicago each cast approximately half of the vote in their states, New Orleans is outweighed three to one in the Louisiana vote. Because of this, the New Orleans machine from the start had little success in electing state officials. The Ring's endorsement always was of doubtful value in state elections.

In the city itself, and in Orleans parish, the machine ruled by means of superior organization, supported in typical fashion by city and parish (county) patronage, by vote frauds in varying degree, and by graft supplied by the purveyors of the various vices that flourished in tolerant, wide-open New Orleans.

Its solid bloc of members in the state legislature, one-quarter of the membership of each house, was strong enough to defend the Ring's interests there. Governors, whether elected with the city organization's support or over its opposition, found it advisable to give the Ring its share of state patronage.

The Regulars never were handicapped by a too strict morality in money matters. Every candidate nominated for elective office was required to pledge ten per cent of his salary as a contribution to the organization. Business enterprises found it advisable to chip in for the support of the dominant political group.

The opposition, consisting mainly of the "silk stocking" elements and the newspapers, was unorganized and ineffective.

The machine's only defeat—right up to the present time—came in 1920, and only then because of unusual circumstances.

In the state election earlier in the same year, John M. Parker, prominent nationally as a Bull Moose ally of Theodore Roosevelt, had been elected governor over the bitter opposition of the machine. Governor Parker, a strong-willed individualist with an appetite for revenge, promptly shut off the Ring's state patronage—a real blow, since the state-controlled New Orleans dock board had, at the time, a particularly luscious gravy bowl in the form of a $30,000,000 appropriation for construction of a ship canal.

John P. Sullivan, national Exalted Ruler of the Elks and one of the crown princes of the Ring, saw in the situation an opportunity to oust Mayor

Behrman and gain control of the organization. Governor Parker gladly contributed to this project by turning over the dock board and other state patronage to Sullivan and the Ring's malcontents who gathered around him.

The combination of a hostile state administration, a split in the city machine and the normal anti-machine vote, proved too much for the Ring. Despite some plain and fancy vote-stealing and the utmost efforts of the police stationed at the polling places, Mayor Behrman was defeated for re-election by the opposition candidate. He was Andrew J. McShane, an "honest" dealer in hides.

The state administration, seeking to consolidate this victory, made a number of changes in the election laws which it confidently expected would "end machine rule" in New Orleans. The registration law was amended to require parish officials to supply to the registrars of voters the names of persons who had died, been sent to the insane asylum or been convicted of crime, so that their names could be removed from the voting lists. The number of tombstones, idiots and convicts voted by the Ring presumably declined as a result, but it had been a minor factor in the first place, and the city machine had no difficulty in making up for the loss in other ways.

The new election law also deprived city officials of the power of assigning policemen to election day duty and vested it in the parish officials instead. The New Orleans Ring, which controlled the Orleans parish election board, was not even seriously inconvenienced in the matter of exercising police influence at the polls. Finally, the new law required candidates to file reports of campaign contributions and expenditures. Both the organization and the opposition simply ignored this provision of the law. Eventually it was nullified by a judicial ruling that it did not apply to primary contests.

The machine was not much hampered by these supposed reforms, as it proved by re-electing Behrman as mayor in 1924. More troublesome was a continuing split in the organization. Paul Maloney, then president of the Choctaw Club and now a member of Congress with machine support, was the unsuccessful candidate of the "New Regulars."

By the time of Behrman's death, two years later, the Sullivan-Maloney faction had been reduced to impotence and the "Old Regulars" were in as firm control as before the split.

Huey Long, the country boy from North Louisiana, made his first bid for the governorship in the same year that Behrman was returned to City Hall. The Old Regulars opposed him.

Mayor Behrman was a Jewish immigrant who had embraced Catholicism. As the political boss in a predominantly Catholic city, with the rest of the state overwhelmingly Protestant, he always had striven to keep the religious line from being drawn in either state or city politics. In 1924, with the Ku Klux Klan a dangerous element in the state, he was particularly careful to avoid creating the basis for an inflammable issue between the Catholics and the Klan. One of the three candidates for governor was a Catholic; the others, both Protestants, were Huey Long and Henry L. Fuqua. Behrman regarded Fuqua as the more tolerant of the two and, largely for that reason, gave him the machine's endorsement.

Huey retaliated with violent, burning attacks on the depravity and corruption of the big city and its political bosses. He made the iniquities of the Ring one of his major issues in the campaign.

The thirty-one-year-old Kingfish ran first by a comfortable margin in the state outside of New Orleans, but he received only eighteen per cent of the vote in the city. With the vote split three ways, Fuqua's plurality in New Orleans was sufficient to elect him.

Huey put the City Hall Ring down as a double starred entry in the S.O.B. book which he was just beginning to compile.

When the Long cyclone finally hit the state with overpowering force in 1928, the boss of the New Orleans machine was T. Semmes Walmsley, who later had the audacity to call Huey "a yellow coward." Walmsley, the city attorney, had been maneuvered into City Hall to complete Behrman's term when Behrman's immediate successor, Arthur J. O'Keefe, Sr., a ward leader in the machine, resigned because of illness.

In the state election in January the Old Regulars supported Congressman Riley Wilson for governor, and carried the city for him by a normal machine vote. Huey Long, with his "Share the Wealth" and "Every Man a King" slogans, polled only 23 per cent of the city vote, but this time his overwhelming plurality in the country parishes was sufficient to elect him.

It was a normal result, so far as the machine was concerned, but Louisiana already was beginning to realize that Huey Long would not be a normal chief executive of the state. The new governor immediately grabbed every job under his control, including those of the dock board, levee board and other state agencies in New Orleans. And he began the process of creating thousands of new patronage jobs through his public works program.

One of the first men whom Long appointed to office was Robert S. Maestri, who was destined eventually to become a worthy successor to Behrman as the boss of New Orleans.

Maestri, a first generation Italian-American, already was one of the wealthiest men in New Orleans. He had figured in politics chiefly as a heavy contributor to the Ring's campaign funds, but in

1928 he had transferred his financial support to Huey Long.

Huey made him head of the conservation department, which controlled the state's oil reserves. In the next few years Maestri greatly enlarged his personal fortune by dealing in oil lands.

By the time the municipal election came around in the Fall of 1928, Governor Long was well entrenched at Baton Rouge and had made progress in his plan to build up an invincible state political organization. But he had not made a dent in the New Orleans machine.

Mayor Walmsley was a candidate for re-election. Opposing him Huey put up Francis Williams, who had been one of Huey's colleagues in the three-man state public service commission years earlier. The Old Regulars polished off the Williams-Long combination without even working up a sweat. It was only a token of what was to come.

Huey was too busy subduing the rest of the state to devote much time to the New Orleans Ring during the next few years. There were a few gestures such as sending the National Guard into the city for a spectacular but soon forgotten campaign to clean out the gamblers. And when the Ring attempted to block his $100,000,000 public works bond issue, Huey held up the city's tax assessment rolls and ordered the Louisiana banks to call city loans.

Huey's grand strategy called for whipping the rest of the state into complete subjection before tackling the real showdown with the city machine, which he recognized as his toughest nut to crack. The leaders of the Ring also could see the inevitable showdown approaching, and were preparing for it.

The big fight came in the next mayoralty election, when Mayor Walmsley sought re-election.

Huey, then a member of the United States Senate, was the absolute dictator of the state government. His "Share the Wealth" movement was becoming a national menace to the Democratic Party. He had demonstrated his power by maneuvering the election of Hattie Caraway to the Senate in neighboring Arkansas. He had boasted that he would take over Mississippi when he was ready, and Mississippi politicians had little doubt that he would do just that.

But Huey, at the height of his power, still couldn't beat the Old Regulars in New Orleans.

As his candidate Huey put up John Klorer, a member of the patronage-inflated dock board. In order to obtain an additional quota of election day watchers and guards, each able to swing a few votes, he put in a "dummy" candidate, as well. Every state agency was mobilized for the fight. State payrolls in the city were built up until they rivaled the municipal payroll.

Mayor Walsmley mobilized the city police to protect the sanctity of the polls. Dictator-Senator Long called out the state militia for the same purpose. With the military forces approximately balanced, both sides agreed to withdraw and leave supervision of the polls to committees of citizens.

When the dust settled, Mayor Walmsley had been re-elected. The Old Regulars still ruled New Orleans.

Unable to beat the machine, Huey declared war on the city government which it controlled. He summoned the state legislature into special session and put it to work grinding out a series of laws which were designed to bring the city administration to its knees. He transferred the city police and fire departments to state control. He took away the city's control of registration books and election machinery, giving custody of the ballot boxes to state election supervisors. He deprived the city of control over its revenues by creating a new branch of the state tax commission to replace the New Orleans board of assessors. The banks were ordered by Dictator Long to call their loans to the city and to refuse any new advances.

What Huey had been unable to accomplish at the polls he achieved through this ruthless and irresistible pressure against the city government. Municipal workers were going without pay. Uncollected garbage lay in the streets. Mayor Walmsley's own city council turned against him. A majority of the Ring's leaders begged the mayor to sue for peace.

Huey had changed his objective, as well as his tactics, after the defeat of his candidate for mayor. From trying to destroy the machine, he had turned to a campaign to beat it into subjection and take it over. His plan was to force Walmsley to resign and to put his own man in as mayor and boss of the city organization.

This plan had been brought close to realization when an assassin's bullet ended Huey P. Long's fantastic career on September 8, 1935.

The elimination of the Kingfish did not relieve the pressure on the New Orleans city administration. Long's men were still in full control of the state government. Even if they had not been, it would have taken years, with the best of intentions, to undo the damage that Huey had done to the city administration.

The resignation of Mayor Walmsley, which followed shortly, just as Huey had planned, was one of the most amazing "deals" that political history affords.

What Walmsley got out of it, if anything, never has been established. What the Old Regulars got was a promise, by the triumvirate which took over the state reins, that the city's powers would be restored if a man picked by the state machine was installed as mayor. The triumvirate which gave this promise consisted of Richard W. Leche, Seymour Weiss and Robert S. Maestri, the latter being the one-time financial supporter of the Ring who had gone over to Huey in the 1928 campaign.

Only after the plan had been worked out in detail and agreed to did the leaders of the city machine learn who was to be their new mayor and political boss. The man was Maestri.

Maestri was a backroom and counting house politician, a man of monosyllables and of more grunts than words. He had no appetite for a campaign for office. But, in Long's Louisiana, his disinclination for campaigning for office offered no insuperable barrier to his holding an office normally filled by election.

The city commissioner of finance, the man in line for succession to the mayoralty, was persuaded to resign; Maestri was appointed in his place; Mayor Walmsley then resigned, and Maestri was mayor.

When the regular mayoralty election came due the following year Maestri flatly refused to run for the office even though he had the support of the Old Regulars and of the still powerful state machine. That presented a slightly more difficult problem, but the ingenuity of the machine leaders, including Maestri himself, was equal to its solution. Maestri's only opponent, an obscure citizen with no hope of election, was "induced" to retire from the race. And with the opposition thus disposed of, Maestri was "certified into office" under a special act of the legislature, without the formality of an election.

It should not be supposed that Mayor Maestri's dislike for seeing his name on a ballot indicated any lack of interest, or ability in the more fundamental aspects of politics. From the moment that he took over the mayor's office at City Hall he made himself, in fact as well as in name, the complete boss of the by then somewhat groggy Old Regulars machine.

The union of the state and city machines which was attained by the elevation of Maestri to the offices of mayor and city boss formed what was, for a time, an unbeatable combination, controlling the whole field of patronage—and graft—in the state.

But there had been a subtle and almost unrecognized shift in the balance of power. Whereas Huey Long had depended for support primarily on the northern country parishes, the post-Long state machine came to rely heavily on the support of the Old Regulars in New Orleans. And, with the country parishes still well in hand, it seemed for a time that Long's successors were even more firmly entrenched in state power than he himself had ever been.

Leche was elected as governor; Earl Long, Huey's not always loving brother, as lieutenant governor. Allen Ellender, who had been Huey's floor leader in the state legislature, was sent to the United States Senate.

The state scandals which broke into the open following the disappearance of James Monroe Smith, president of the University of Louisiana, in June, 1939, wrecked the state machine, but they left the New Orleans organization untouched.

Leche and Weiss went to jail, as did "Doc" Smith and some dozen underlings of the state organization.

"Doc" Smith had been gambling in the stock market, and had poured $500,000 in state funds down that drain. Leche and Weiss, among other things, had split $134,000 for letting their friends run "hot oil" out of the state. In all, "Dick" Leche had taken in $450,000 in various forms of graft during his three years as governor.

Mayor Maestri's big years, so far as the record showed, had come earlier in the game, while Huey was still governor. The future city boss, as conservation commissioner, had made $1,157,000 in two years from the oil business, including some "hot oil" deals such as those for which Governor Leche and Seymour Weiss later collected heavy "fees."

But Attorney General Frank Murphy and special United States Attorney John Rogge decided that there was no basis for a federal indictment of Mayor Maestri. Some cynics called the decision on Maestri the "Third Louisiana Purchase."

In the meantime "Frankie" Costello, New York City racketeer and Tammany political fixer, had moved the headquarters of his slot machine syndicate to New Orleans after Mayor LaGuardia drove the gambling devices out of New York. With his partner, "Jimmy" Moran, who had been a friend of Huey Long, Costello grossed $2,500,000 in two years from the slot machines. He and "Jimmy" became intimate friends of Mayor Maestri.

By the time the state election came around in 1940, the old state machine founded by Huey Long had been completely broken up. Its top leaders were in jail or the federal penitentiary. The lesser ones were scurrying around, looking for the best bandwagon on which to jump. Only the New Orleans Old Regulars remained virtually untouched, still in complete control of the city government.

Mayor Maestri, hoping to capitalize on the Long worship which still persisted in north Louisiana, to extend the Ring's control to the state government, backed Earl Long for the nomination for governor.

The reform elements and newspapers united behind Sam Houston Jones, the chamber of commerce reform candidate.

Several other candidates entered the face. One of them was "Jimmy" Noe, who had become lieutenant governor after Huey installed O. K. Allen as his successor in the governor's chair. "Jimmy" Noe had harbored a deep and burning resentment against the other Long heirs since they passed over him to support "Dick" Leche for governor after Huey's assassination. He had helped bring to light the scandals of the Leche administration.

Another candidate was James H. Morrison, an energetic young lawyer who had made a study of Huey's methods and idiosyncrasies and then set out to emulate, or surpass, Huey's career.

Earl Long, the machine's candidate, led the field in the primary returns, with "Sam" Jones second and "Jimmy" Noe third. But since no candidate had a majority, a run-off election was necessary between Earl Long and Jones. "Jimmy" Noe, willing to support the devil against Earl Long, threw his support, and most of his votes, to Sam Jones.

Earl Long, the Dictator's brother, lost the country parishes, where Huey always had been supreme, but the Old Regulars delivered New Orleans, which Huey never had been able to carry against the machine.

Sam Jones, the reformer, won the election by a plurality of 17,000 votes.

Louisiana politics was about back to normal—

with only some new faces here and there to show for the upheaval that had been accomplished by Huey Long.

In the mayoralty campaign later in the year Maestri—finally persuaded to let his name appear on the city ballot—was re-elected by the Old Regulars after a bitter, knock-down and drag out fight in which the "reform" state administration and the newspapers backed his principal opponent.

Voting machines were used for the first time in the mayoralty election, and opponents of the Old Regulars had high hopes that the Ring would be so handicapped in its ballot-box stuffing operations that much of its advantage would be lost.

But the Old Regulars were not to be outdone by mere mechanical devices. The law under which the voting machines were installed provided that voters who were illiterate or physically incapable of operating the machines could request assistance in casting their ballots. The Ring obtained from the city attorney an "opinion" that this provision permitted any voter to call for assistance.

Under this liberal opinion, still more liberally interpreted at many of the polling places, the Old Regulars' representatives at the polls were enabled to exercise as great a degree of supervision as ever over the voting by city employes, their relatives, and other followers of the machine.

Members of the Old Regulars estimate that the

organization can control about 40,000 votes out of the normal total of 102,000 or 103,000 votes cast in the city. This ability to cast approximately forty per cent of the vote one way or the other is, of course, the ability to control the result of the election, except under highly unusual conditions.

The state election on January 18, 1944—a free-for-all fight between eight full tickets—failed to result in a clear majority for any candidates, necessitating a run-off election later in the year.

Of 105,000 votes in Orleans parish, the machine candidates received from 50,000 to 55,000 votes, their pluralities ranging from 17,000 to 26,000 over the second highest candidates.

Lewis L. Morgan, the Old Regulars' candidate for governor, ran a bad second in the country parishes and finished up 35,000 votes behind hill-billy-crooner Jimmie H. Davis, political heir of the Jones reform administration, in the state totals. But four of the Maestri-backed candidates, including Earl Long, candidate for lieutenant governor, won first place in the voting and seemed likely to be elected in the run-off.

Thus the Old Regulars, still dominant in the city, seemed to be fastening their grip on at least a portion of the state government.

9

ALABAMA BOUND

THE OLD SOUTH, with its slave-holding psychology and its conservative ruling class governing behind the protection of the one-party system and the poll tax, has become a generally accepted symbol for Bourbon rule in modern America.

In the past when the Solid South has kicked over the traces against the rule of its "better classes," it usually has managed to produce only crackpots and rabble-rousers, or demagogues such as "Tom" Watson and "Gene" Talmadge of Georgia, "Tom-Tom" Heflin and Frank Dixon of Alabama, Cole Blease of South Carolina, "The Man" Bilbo of Mississippi, and "Pappy" O'Daniel of Texas. Even a period of eleven years during which the nation's affairs have been conducted by a liberal Democratic administration in Washington has produced few apparent changes in the political lineup in the deep South.

In two states, however, the national ferment,

operating despite the restrictions of one-party, poll-tax politics, has brought to the top two genuine Rooseveltian liberals. They are United States Senators Claude Pepper of Florida and Lister Hill of Alabama. And, being better than average politicians, both of them have taken good care of their political fences back home.

The Lister Hill political machine in Alabama is less a political machine, in the ordinary sense of the word, than it is a network of key individuals and groups which covers the state and which can be thrown into action to support a state-wide political program.

Alabama for years has wavered between two extremes in the character of its officials. It has had in the Senate, at the same time, the able, scholarly, highly conservative Oscar W. Underwood, for whom Alabama cast twenty-four votes for the presidential nomination on so many ballots at the 1924 Democratic national convention, and J. Thomas "Tom-Tom" Heflin, the anti-Negro, anti-Catholic rabble-rouser. It is represented in the Senate now by the liberal Lister Hill and the conservative John H. Bankhead. It even has produced in one and the same person—Hugo L. Black—a former member of the Ku Klux Klan who lived to become the Supreme Court's most determined present-day defender of civil liberties and the rights of minority groups. Mr. Justice Black, as will appear, helped to lay the foundation on which the present Lister Hill organization was constructed.

The story of present day politics in Alabama starts in 1925 when Senator Underwood, unsuccessful in his ambition to run for the presidency but garlanded with the glories of thirty years of useful service in Congress, decided to retire to private life and write his memoirs.

The Ku Klux Klan, resurrected by self-seeking racketeers from its grave in the history of Reconstruction days, was riding high in the early 1920's. Its power in politics was felt not only in its birthplace and stronghold in the deep South, but notably in such non-Southern states as Indiana, Maine and Oregon. Viciously lawless, anti-Catholic as well as anti-Negro, founded on ignorance and superstition, Klanism in America was a precursor and close relative of Naziism in Germany. In 1924 the night-shirted Klan had been dragged onto the floor of the Democratic national convention in New York's Madison Square Garden, and Democrats from all over the country had argued passionately for two days over whether or not they could afford to "name" the Klan in a platform declaration against bigotry and intolerance. That debate struck a heavy blow at the Klan, but the hooded organization lingered on as a potent political force for several years.

In Alabama the Klan ruled the state. Many of the "best people" were members. Politicians and storekeepers found it necessary to join in order to stay in business. The "nice people" mildly deplored the terroristic beatings and other forms of hoodlumism indulged in by their hooded fellow-Klansmen. But they supported the hoodlums and condoned their actions by continued membership in the secret order.

Senator Underwood was the South's most prominent political figure of his day, perhaps its leading statesman of the present century. But he had opposed the Ku Klux Klan, and the Klan had marked him for defeat. The senator shrank from a campaign in which all of the Klan's venom would have been turned against him. And he was doubtless tired of the company of his Senate colleague, the demagogic "Tom-Tom" Heflin. When Underwood's decision not to seek re-election became known, John Bankhead became a candidate for the Democratic nomination in the party primary which was, and still is, the real election in Alabama.

The Bankhead family already was a political institution in the state. The candidate's father, John H. Bankhead I, had been prominent in Alabama from the time he shed his Confederate captain's uniform in 1865. He had been a member of the United States Senate from 1907 until his death in 1920. One of his sons, William B. Bankhead, later to become Speaker of the House of Representatives, had been a member of the House since 1916. John II looked like a sure bet to make it a family grand slam by being elected as Underwood's successor in 1926. But a young, politically unknown Birmingham lawyer, unimpressed by the Bankhead family tree, had his own analysis of the situation. And he had plenty of ambition, energy and ability.

Hugo Black had come back from the war a few years earlier, resumed his Birmingham practice where he had left off in 1917, and was doing very well for a youngster in his thirties. His income, derived chiefly from trial of personal injury damage suits, was running around $35,000 or $40,000 a year. But he confidently closed his office, bought a second-hand automobile, and started out, a year in advance of the 1926 primary, to win the Democratic nomination for United States Senator. He had worn out two cars, talked to every voter in the state and joined every available lodge and society, including the Ku Klux Klan, before the Bankhead supporters realized that he was really to be taken seriously. By then it was too late. Black, the political unknown, went to the Senate; Bankhead put his toga away in moth balls for four years.

At the same time Bibb Graves, one of the most cheerful and appealing political frauds of modern times, was elected governor of Alabama. Graves, like Black, had Klan support in his campaign. Otherwise there was no connection between the senatorial and gubernatorial elections. But in retrospect the elections of Governor Graves and Senator Black can be linked as marking the joint beginnings of the organization later led by Lister Hill, who became the chief political heir of both. Hill himself was not to emerge as a state figure for many years. In 1926 he was thirty-two years old and had been a member of Congress from the Montgomery district for three years. He wasn't very prominent on the national stage in Washington, but he was hard at work on the political fundamentals involved in holding his job and building for the future. In other words, Hill was doing little favors for hundreds of his constituents, writing thousands of letters, getting a job for someone in his district now and then, and always keeping his eyes open for any possible pork barrel items in the way of federally financed public improvements for the district.

Bibb Graves' inauguration as governor was followed by a wild spree for the whole state of Alabama. Anyone who wanted a job could have one at the capitol in Montgomery. Hundreds of people were on the state payroll who never worked for even a day. Their checks were mailed to them. The governor allowed his lawyer friends to buy pardons and paroles for convicts. He poured money into the public highway system and much of it was either wasted or stolen. Graves also believed in public education—and in the political value of having the teachers (a strong political group in Alabama) on his side. There is a Bibb Graves Hall on every college campus in Alabama.

Governor Graves was so thoroughly a machine politician at heart, and had practiced the art of politics so long, that he saw nothing wrong in rewarding his politically faithful friends in every possible way. He couldn't understand why the newspapers howled about corruption and waste. The reason he had run for office was that he had wanted to be in a position to help his friends. And he was willing to be friends with anyone who would be on his side.

Graves apparently could have remained as governor for the rest of his life if it had not been for a provision in the Alabama constitution which prohibits a governor from succeeding himself. As it was, he had to retire, temporarily, on the completion of his four-year term in 1930. He went out of office the most popular, as well as the most hated, governor in the state's history. He was sure of re-election four years later.

Meanwhile, Senator Heflin had outguessed himself in the 1928 presidential campaign, when Al Smith's nomination for the presidency had split the Southern Democracy down the middle. Ro-

manism always had been one of Heflin's favorite
bogeys. He bolted the Smith ticket. Alabama almost followed him into the Hoover camp, but
when the senator came up for renomination two
years later the passions of the 1928 campaign had
been forgotten. Everything, that is, except the un-
deniable, unpardonable and damning fact that
Heflin had run out on his party. The same Ala-
bamians who had voted against Smith turned
around two years later and voted against Heflin
because he had opposed Smith.

The beneficiaries were John H. Bankhead II,
who finally realized his ambition to be elected to
the Senate, and Senator Black, who saw Bankhead's
election as removing a dangerous rival for his own
seat in 1932.

Black already had begun to carve himself a place
in the Senate as a leader of liberal thought and
policies. He had joined Senator George Norris, of
Nebraska, in fighting for public development and
operation of the power resources at Muscle Shoals
in northern Alabama. This was a popular issue in
Black's state, where the Alabama Power Company
had been exploiting the publicly owned but pri-
vately distributed Muscle Shoals power at the
expense of utility consumers. When Black came
up for re-election in 1932, Governor Roosevelt
was running for President, with public development of power as one of his big issues. Black was

opposed by former Governor Thomas E. Kilby, but he tied himself to Roosevelt's coat tails and was re-elected easily.

The inauguration of a Democratic President and national administration gave both Alabama senators an opportunity further to entrench themselves with the voters. Black consolidated his liberal following, particularly in Birmingham, where the newspapers have been less reactionary than in most Southern cities, by his sponsorship of measures such as the thirty-hour week, spread-the-work bill. And he reaped most of the credit, back home, for passage of the TVA act.

Bankhead from the start had set out to make himself the farmers' friend, realizing that if he could get the farmers behind him, he would be safe for life. As a member of the Senate Agriculture Committee, he was in an ideal position to capitalize on the Roosevelt administration's farm policies. He introduced several of the administration's farm bills and played a leading part in passage of the original Agricultural Adjustment Act. As the price of cotton rose steadily from its depression low of five cents a pound, Bankhead's stock with Alabama farmers went up correspondingly.

Both senators also had the opportunity to make numerous federal appointments during the early New Deal days. Black used this opportunity to build up a network of young, progressive-minded officeholders in spots around the state where they could be of influence in future campaigns.

Bankhead, relying on his solid farm support to keep him in office, used his patronage power in a more personal way. The family was well taken care of. The senator's son-in-law, Charles Crow, was appointed as clerk of the Federal Court in Birmingham. And some of Bankhead's successful candidates for judicial appointment have been notably partial to the senator's law firm, headed by his son, Walter Will Bankhead, in the awarding of bankruptcy cases and other court patronage. Walter Will, needless to say, became one of the most successful and wealthiest lawyers in Alabama.

For re-election purposes, Bankhead built up a strong rural organization through the extension service of the Department of Agriculture, which is controlled locally rather than from Washington, and through the American Farm Bureau Federation, which is closely connected with the extension service.

There are about one thousand employes in the sixty-seven county offices of the extension service, which allots acreage for basic crops and distributes government hand-out checks. The county agent is the head of this organization in each county. In addition to his staff of employes, he appoints in each county a Triple-A committee, composed of old established farmers who think pretty much as the county agent does. These assignments are valuable. The committee members get a special gasoline allotment for every county meeting and are paid on a per diem basis when they are attending the meetings. The patronage possibilities in such a setup are obvious.

In Alabama (not an isolated instance), the generally anti-New Deal Farm Bureau Federation has knit itself closely into the operations of the extension service. Often, when government farm checks are being handed out, a Farm Bureau man is on hand in the county agent's office to demand payment of federation dues. In the more backward areas the federation takes credit for the government handouts. In some cases, with the connivance of the county agents a check-off system has been instituted by which federation dues are automatically deducted from government benefit checks, and the farmers, willy nilly, become members of the Farm Bureau Federation.

Thus the Farm Bureau Federation, a private, wholly unofficial pressure group, uses the government benefits, instituted by the Roosevelt administration, to build a formidable political organization, the machinery of which is in the hands of men who for the most part are inimical to all of the Roosevelt domestic program, except for the farm handouts.

Senator Bankhead almost completely controls this organization in Alabama so far as he wants to use it to advance his own political fortunes. He must, and does, exercise that control cautiously, however. The political line cuts through the farm population. In the South, particularly, the small independent farmers, tenant farmers and farm workers have a strong personal loyalty to President Roosevelt. Any attempt to use the farm organization openly and directly against the President would split the Bankhead machine and destroy its power. But it can be, and is, used slyly to oppose his objectives.

The conservative big business interests in the state—what Bibb Graves labeled the Birmingham "Big Mules"—work hand in glove with the Farm Bureau Federation. The Associated Industries of Alabama, a branch of the National Association of Manufacturers, is a well organized and well financed political force when it wishes to get into a campaign. The state Chamber of Commerce, dominated by the Alabama Power Company, is equally active in politics. As usual in the cases of big business groups in politics, both organizations can supply more money and organizing talent than they can votes. With the spreading network of the Farm Bureau Federation, they form the backbone of the Bankhead organization.

The election of Bibb Graves in 1934 for a second

four-year term as governor opened the way for the revival and strengthening of the patronage and spoils organization which he had founded during his first term from 1926 to 1930.

The newspapers, which had futilely exposed the corruption of the first Graves administration, were solidly lined up against him in 1934, but they had little effect in dimming his popularity.

"Those who help us bake the pie will help us eat it," Graves promised in a sincere and homely adaptation of the slogan: "To the victors belong the spoils." The newspapers tried to use that promise against him, but those who were helping Graves win knew that they would eat the pie, and they stuck to him.

Once again the state payrolls were violently expanded and state funds were poured out in the formation of a state-wide patronage machine of municipal and county officers, teachers and education officials.

During all of this period, Lister Hill was solidifying his own support in his Congressional district, which included Montgomery, the state capital. In Hill's own words, he has "been running for office every day" since he got out of the University of Alabama Law School in 1915 and opened an office in Montgomery. He was elected president of the Montgomery Board of Education in 1917. The World War, in which he served as an infantry officer, interrupted his political career only temporarily. In 1923, at the age of twenty-eight, he was elected to Congress, where he served continuously for fifteen years.

Hill's record in the House was that of a progressive and, after 1933, of a New Dealer. But it was not a particularly distinguished record. Hill was too busy looking after his constituents and his district. His success in having Montgomery selected as the site for Maxwell Field, now one of the principal Army Air Force training centers, meant much more in votes than did Hill's consistent support of the TVA legislation.

When President Roosevelt got his first opportunity to fill a vacancy on the United States Supreme Court and selected Senator Black for the post, the question of a successor to Black in the Senate was discussed at the White House. The President and Black agreed on Hill as the best man for the post. Mr. Roosevelt picked up the telephone and called Governor Graves, who would have the appointive power to fill the Senate vacancy. Graves agreed, with the proviso, which was accepted, that he would name his wife, Dixie Bibb Graves, as senator for the balance of 1937. Hill was in Europe at the time, with the American Battle Monuments Commission, dedicating memorials to American dead in France and Belgium. His candidacy was agreed on before he was ever consulted, and announced while he was still abroad.

The President's selection of Hill made him at least one powerful enemy in the Alabama delegation in Congress. Representative Henry B. Steagall, who died in 1943, had Senate ambitions, and he never got over his resentment that the President had decided against his claims. As the influential chairman of the House Banking and Currency Committee, Steagall threw many hurdles in the path of the administration's legislative program thereafter. Senator Bankhead undoubtedly shared the feelings of Steagall, with whom he had a close political relationship based on mutual support. But the necessity for living together within the confines of a one-party political setup prevented any open Alabama split. Hill, Bankhead and Steagall remained mutually friendly, although frequently working at political cross purposes.

Hill first was elected to the Senate in April, 1938, after the anti-Roosevelt forces in the state had failed to develop a strong candidate against him. "Tom-Tom" Heflin ran against him, but the Klan, Heflin's power in earlier days, was gone, and Heflin's day had passed. The Montgomery *Advertiser*, reluctantly supporting Hill as the lesser of two evils, said succinctly: "Heflin is Heflin—a buffoon and a hogbladder."

Hill had the solid support of Senator Black's sketchy organization, which he took over, and he had the backing, too, of the state machine headed by Governor Graves. From these two groups Hill, since his election to the Senate, has built up his present state-wide New Deal machine.

Senator Hill has used his patronage opportunities to good political advantage. Throughout Alabama there has been created a network of active, alert federal officeholders who owe their appointments to Hill. Most of them are young; all of them are personally loyal to Hill. Most of them are political progressives. Although the Hatch Act prohibits their formal participation in political activities, they are, in fact, a strong political force in their communites and in the state.

The principal figure in this group is Roy Nolen, for many years Hill's campaign manager and political agent, who is now postmaster of Montgomery. Nolen is rated in Alabama as a shrewd political strategist and a skillful practical politician. Others in the Hill strategy board are Marc Ray Clement, political leader of Tuscaloosa County and chairman of the War Fund drive in Alabama, and Clarence Allgood, referee in bankruptcy in the Birmingham federal court district.

Another influential Hill appointee is Albert C. Collins, state director of the Office of Price Administration. Collins, a leader in Alabama liberal politics, was retiring as state superintendent of education in 1942, just as Leon Henderson, head of the Office of Price Administration, was building up his state and regional OPA organization. Senator Hill proposed Collins as Alabama OPA director.

Henderson was taking recommendations for state appointees from governors rather than senators (a practice which contributed to his eventual downfall) but Hill insisted on Collins getting the job. Collins was, to borrow a senatorial phrase, "personally repugnant" to Frank M. Dixon, then governor of Alabama. A direct showdown of patronage power resulted—and Collins got the job.

The real working part of the Hill machine is based on his political strength with the teachers and the municipal officials, two of the most potent organized political groups in Alabama. In both cases the roots of the Hill organization stem back to the state machine built up by Governor Graves. (Graves died just as he was preparing to run for his third term as governor in 1942.)

The teachers are organized in the Alabama Education Association. While the A.E.A. does not formally endorse candidates, there is seldom a campaign when it is not well known for whom the school forces are lined up. The leaders know the side their bread is buttered on, and it does not take much effort on their part to pass the word down the line. Political writers for the newspapers always can state with confidence which candidates the school forces are supporting.

Albert C. Collins, the OPA director, is still one of the political leaders of the teachers' group. Another is Dr. Henry J. Willingham, former president of Florence State Teachers' College, whose political activity was rewarded when he was appointed as federal collector of internal revenue for Alabama.

In addition to the grade and high school forces, the "big three" in higher education—University of Alabama, Alabama Polytechnic Institute at Auburn and Alabama College for Women at Montevallo—are all active in politics.

Dr. L. N. Duncan, president of Auburn, figures in politics in a dual capacity. In addition to his educational affiliations, he is the real boss of the Department of Agriculture's extension service, which operates from Auburn under the general supervision of the college authorities. Thus, Dr. Duncan's symathies are divided between the generally liberal teachers' groups and the reactionary lobbyists who run the Farm Bureau Federation.

The second and equally important pillar of the Hill machine is the Alabama League of Municipalities, a strong and cohesive organization of all the state's mayors and city commissioners. The municipal officials have been overwhelmingly pro-Roosevelt and pro-Graves, and Hill is the inheritor of that support.

Ed E. "Eddie" Reid, executive secretary of the

League of Municipalities, is its active head, with headquarters in Montgomery. He is an exceptionally able political organizer, and he knows how to "deliver." When a mayor needs help in Washington, for example, Reid gets it through Senator Hill's office. As a result, the municipal officials are with Hill almost unanimously. Each of the municipal officers has his own local organization, which becomes, in time of need, a part of the Hill state machine.

There has been no direct test of strength at the primaries between the Hill and Bankhead organizations. They probably are about evenly balanced. In any event, each senator has found it advisable to stay on good terms with the other, rather than to permit their totally different political philosophies to bring them into a conflict which would eventually result in the elimination of one or the other.

The existence of the strong Hill organization in the cities and towns possibly tempers Bankhead's opposition to many of the policies of the Roosevelt administration. It would be virtually political suicide for Bankhead to bolt either the Roosevelt or the Democratic ticket, as some of his fellow conservative Southern Democrats have talked of doing.

And, by the same token, the existence of Bankhead's strong rural organization makes it advisable for Senator Hill, the New Dealer, to trim his sails to meet the views of the anti-Roosevelt lobby run by the big farm-owning interests.

Hill, the politician, has carefully seen to it that his voting record on farm bills, ever since he went to the Senate in January, 1938, has been identical with Bankhead's.

10

AFTER PENDERGAST

"THE BIGGER they are, the harder they fall," is an adage as true in politics as it is in the prize ring. Thomas J. Pendergast, one-time boss of Kansas City and of Missouri, now an ex-convict living in retirement in Kansas City under threat of being sent back to jail if he engages in any political activity, is a classic example.

No other private individual has ever so completely dominated the government of a state as Boss Tom did that of Missouri during the height of his power from 1932 to 1938. During that period not a single state official was elected without having first received the nod from Boss Pendergast. And once elected they all—with one final and fatal exception—did the boss' bidding. The state legislature, the governor and all lesser elective state officials were under Tom Pendergast's thumb. No appointments to state jobs were made without his sanction.

Pendergast's dingy office on the second floor of a small two-story building at 1908 Main Street, near Kansas City's Union Station, came to be known as the "Capitol of Missouri." The official state capitol in Jefferson City was called "Uncle Tom's Cabin."

During the same period, and for many years before his final ascendancy in the state, Pendergast ruled the municipal government of Kansas City with the same thoroughness.

All that was swept away in a brief two-year period by a calculated, systematic job of civic reform that was as carefully planned and executed as anything the boss himself had ever engineered. Ironically, Governor Lloyd C. Stark, who did the job, had been put into office by the Pendergast machine.

By the end of 1939 Pendergast and a group of his puppets, several of them public officials, had been sent to the Federal penitentiary at Leavenworth, Kansas, for failure to report bribery receipts on their Federal income tax returns; some 60,000 "ghost" names had been stricken from the Kansas City registration lists where they had been fraudulently placed and voted by the Pendergast machine; scores of little Pendergast election officials had been jailed or fined for vote frauds; a police-underworld alliance in Kansas City had been exposed and broken up, and the city itself had been transformed from a wide open resort for gambling and vice into a "Sunday School" community.

Today there is no political machine worthy of the name anywhere in Missouri. The Democratic Party has lost the governorship, and its state organization is weak and divided. There is no head of Democratic politics in Kansas City. Municipal politics in Pendergast's city are run by a bi-partisan "clean up" group which controls the city administration. Nor is there any effective organization in St. Louis, where a budding machine was nipped in 1940.

The Republicans are little better off. There are GOP factions, each with some strength, but none of them even approaches dominance. There is no Republican machine in the sense of an organization able to control elections.

II

The machine that came to be controlled entirely by the arrogant, bulldog-jawed Tom Pendergast had a small beginning nearly forty years ago in the activities of Tom's older brother, James, who organized Democratic politics in the "West Bottoms," in Kansas City's First ward. It was a neighborhood of factories, flop houses and big five-cent beers.

Jim Pendergast, as a ward political leader in that sort of neighborhood, naturally became a saloonkeeper, opening a place on Main Street on the North Side. Oldtimers say that he ran a "decent" saloon. Many an election in the First ward was fixed in the back room, but Jim was a law-abiding citizen according to his lights, and he ran an orderly place. When a customer had "enough" he got no more to drink, and if he became obstreperous Jim was man enough to throw him out without calling for help.

Jim followed the regular rule for political bosses. Nobody suffered from cold or hunger in the First ward. If they didn't have the money to buy coal and food Jim saw to it that they got such necessities of life. Gradually everybody in the First ward voted as Jim told them to vote, or, if they didn't, their votes were counted that way. He might permit an opposing candidate to have five or ten votes recorded for him, while the Pendergast candidate showed up with 1,000 or 1,500. There was no doubt about it—Jim could deliver the First ward.

He was elected an alderman, and then began to branch out. His younger brother, Tom, was coming along and showing much aptitude for politics. Tom could handle the little details of the First ward and help out in other places as Jim gradually extended his practices and influence to other parts of the city and even into Jackson County, the larger political unit in which Kansas City is situated.

At that time the Number One Democratic politician in Kansas City, something of a boss himself, was Joseph B. Shannon, long afterward a member of Congress. Pendergast began worming into the Shannon-controlled wards, and there developed a bitter rivalry between the Shannon "rabbits" and the Pendergast "goats," as they were called. Pendergast was skillful in political maneuvers. As he gradually gained, the Shannon faction weakened, until they were fairly evenly divided in political strength when Jim Pendergast died in 1916.

Tom Pendergast took over the expanding machine. He had been schooled in his brother's methods and was even more ambitious than Jim had been to build a strong political organization. Those were the days of mass primaries, and there were frequent slugging matches between the Pendergast and Shannon followers. Sometimes there were killings. Almost always there were bloody fights.

There came a time when Pendergast and Shannon divided the jobs in the City Hall and the County Court House on almost an even basis; and finally there was an agreement that Pendergast would have two-thirds of the jobs and Shannon one-third. In his two-thirds Pendergast, however, was forced to take care of a small organization dominated by Casimer J. Welsh, a justice of the peace, known as the leader of the "Fifteenth Street boys."

Tom was not satisfied with this arrangement. With his increase in power his arrogance had increased, and with it his determination to control not only Kansas City, but the state as well. He smarted over the necessity of having to divide the patronage spoils with Shannon. A solution did not prove difficult.

Shannon had the feeling that he was a statesman rather than a politician. He wanted to go to Congress, where he could make speeches about Thomas Jefferson and otherwise participate in national affairs.

Pendergast was not much concerned with national affairs, although, of course, he always had his hand in the selection of congressmen and United States senators, and in picking the delegates to the Democratic national conventions. But those things did not mean many jobs, and it was on jobs that Pendergast relied for his power.

So it was agreed that Shannon should go to Congress with Pendergast's blessing. He was elected in 1930 and thereby shelved, as far as Missouri political influence was concerned, for twelve years, until his death in 1942.

This made Pendergast supreme in Kansas City. The leaders of the old Shannon "rabbits" received some consideration from Pendergast to keep them quiet, but in the main the Shannon crowd backed Pendergast in whatever he decided.

During most of this time there was only a semblance of a Republican organization in Kansas City. Frequently there were "deals" between the controlling influences among the Republicans and Pendergast, by which Pendergast got a free hand in primary elections, and many of the GOP ward leaders were permitted crumbs from the boss' table.

With his ability to control a sizeable block of votes, Tom Pendergast had begun to be recognized as a power in state politics from 1916 on. Every Democratic candidate for state office made his pilgrimage to the little office at 1908 Main Street, where Pendergast held court. All the candidates saw Tom, pleaded for his support, and were curtly told yes or no. Many were the fledgling candidates who withdrew from the race when the boss announced his "no."

Kansas City elections are under the supervision of a Board of Election Commissioners appointed by the governor. From 1921 until 1933, during the period of national GOP ascendancy, Missouri had Republican governors, but that did not interfere with Pendergast's steady march toward power. The law required that there be two Republicans and two Democrats on the election board. Through his virtual control of the state senate, Pendergast could interfere seriously with any governor's program. Most of the Republican governors decided it to be good policy to appoint machine Democrats to the election board in Kansas City. In several instances the Republicans appointed to the board also were under Pendergast's influence.

As the Democratic organization continued to grow in power, the size of the Democratic primary vote increased out of all proportion to the population of the city. It was evident to everybody interested in Missouri politics that the registration lists in Kansas City were heavily padded.

The following tabulation shows the total Democratic and Republican primary vote in Jackson County, which consists of Kansas City and a rural area surrounding it, for each presidential election year since 1916. The figures, covering the period of the rise, complete dominance and final destruction of the Pendergast machine, tell a fascinating story all in themselves:

TOTAL PRIMARY VOTE

	Democratic	Republican	Total
1916	22,809	11,299	34,108
1920	17,000	16,175	33,175
1924	51,368	31,936	83,304
1928	56,043	43,655	99,698
1932	113,198	30,315	143,513
1936	173,194	28,177	201,371
1940	105,487	23,079	128,566

The big jump in the vote between 1920 and 1924 reflected the newly won suffrage of women. But there was no such simple explanation for the skyrocketing of the Democratic vote in 1932 and 1936. The 1930 census showed Jackson County with a population of 470,454, and this figure was virtually unchanged in 1940, when the census showed a population of 477,828. Thus, without any material increase in population, the total primary vote increased from 99,698 in 1928 to 201,371 in 1936, more than doubling. The precipitous drop in the vote in 1940, from the high in 1936, reflected the purging of the registration rolls during that period.

Between 1928 and 1936 the combined Democratic and Republican primary vote in the state outside of Kansas City and Jackson County increased from 721,068 to 833,711, an increase of 15.6 per cent. The Democratic primary vote in the same area increased from 390,300 to 547,519, a rise of 40 per cent.

But in Kansas City and Jackson County the increase in the Democratic primary vote was 209 per cent, a clear indication of the padded lists in Kansas City.

In the tabulation above it is noteworthy that in the Roosevelt years from 1932 to 1936, while the Democratic primary vote in Jackson County was increasing at a tremendous rate, the Republican primary vote fell only slightly. So the Democratic increase did not come from the Republican ranks. It came chiefly from the heavily padded registration lists.

No Democrat opposed by Pendergast was nominated for state office from 1930 until 1938, when the state became aroused over his attempt to invade the state Supreme Court by dictating the nomination of a judge. The registration lists in Kansas City had been purged by that time, and the boss was short some 60,000 votes.

Through the 'twenties, Pendergast had begun developing some strength among the leaders of the court house rings in a number of rural counties, but he had not made great progress until 1932. That year there arose a situation in Missouri which enabled the Kansas City boss to build his state organization and to win control of all elective and appointive offices in the state.

Following the 1930 census, Congress, in its reapportionment act, reduced the number of Missouri representatives in Congress from sixteen to thirteen. This necessitated a redistricting of the state. The legislature of 1931 passed a redistricting act, but it was vetoed by the Republican governor, Henry S. Caulfield, on the ground that it was a Democratic gerrymander. The governor expected that a fairer act would be passed, one that he would sign.

Pendergast, who was alert to the political possibilities, controlled the state senate, and there was no new redistricting act. This meant that the thirteen congressmen had to be nominated and elected at large by the vote of the entire state.

There were fifty-six candidates for the thirteen Democratic nominations. Each of the fifty-six called at 1908 Main Street to get the blessing of the boss. Each was met with this statement: "All right, you want my support. Go back home and see what you can do for me. Upon the information I get I'll decide about you."

Pendergast had a candidate for every state office and, with very few exceptions, each of the fifty-six congressional aspirants went home and began lining up strength for the Pendergast candidates for state offices, particularly for his candidate for governor, Francis M. Wilson. The boss eventually announced his slate for Congress and only one candidate not on the list was nominated.

The candidate for governor died shortly before the election and it then devolved on the Democratic State Committee to name his successor. Pendergast, having shown his power, absolutely controlled the committee. It named Guy B. Park, a judge in a rural circuit bordering on Jackson County. There was no question about Park's obligation to Pendergast. He was governor solely because Pendergast ordered it. A politician out-and-out, Park believed in paying political debts in full, and did so.

A Pendergast man from Kansas City was named State Insurance Superintendent. A Pendergast man from Kansas City was named chairman of the State Public Service Commission. A Pendergast man from Kansas City was named State Liquor Supervisor. All these were jobs which were important to a political boss. As it later developed, they were of particular importance to Pendergast. The boss' men were placed in important jobs in almost every state department, all elective officials having gone into office with his support.

The Park administration was a Pendergast administration. The boss dictated the appointments to the Board of Election Commissioners in Kansas City, and the way was open for whatever the boss wanted in politics. While perhaps he did not actually dictate similar state appointments in St. Louis, the fact was that no one opposed by the boss was named there.

A period of unbridled license followed in Kansas City, which became known as one of the most wide open towns of the United States. Evidence later obtained showed clearly that a direct alliance existed between the police and big-time criminals. Unsolved murders were numerous. The lowest forms of vice were carried on openly. It was a great period for the political boss, who made big money through bribes and rake-offs on public contracts, if not in other ways.

But in the next campaign, in 1936, Boss Pendergast made his big mistake—the one which led to his undoing.

Lloyd C. Stark, a wealthy Missourian from Pike County, had decided in 1933 that he wanted to be governor. He began a systematic campaign which he conducted for three years throughout the state and succeeded in building up a strong personal following. Finally Stark made the customary visit to 1908 Main Street, and there received the pledge of Pendergast's support.

The Stark men have always said—since the open break which followed his election—that Pendergast did not want to support Stark and did so only because he knew Stark had the nomination sewed up. Boss Pendergast's partisans, on the other hand, have based their bitter charges of "ingratitude" against Stark on the contention that he, like all other Democratic office holders of that day, owed his place entirely to the boss' favor. In any event, Stark had the full support of the Pendergast machine, and won the nomination.

Boss Pendergast, himself, drunk with power and considering himself invincible, took full credit for Stark's election. He had no doubt that Stark would take his orders, but in that he was wrong. Stark, a graduate of the United States Naval Academy, a

naval officer for a number of years, and chairman
of the board of the Stark Brothers Nursery, a large
business, was accustomed to giving, not taking,
orders.

Shortly after the election Pendergast announced
that he would have only two requests to make of
the governor: one, to have his insurance superintendent under Governor Park continued in office,
and the other, to have a man of his selection named
as chairman of the Public Service Commission.

Governor-elect Stark said nothing; but when he
took office in January, 1937, he named an anti-
Pendergast man to head the Public Service Commission. The term of the insurance superintendent
did not expire until July.

In the summer of that year Stark met Pendergast
in Colorado Springs. He suggested that they discuss
the membership of the Kansas City Board of Election commissioners. The governor replied that he
would attend to that matter without suggestions
from Pendergast. The boss bit his lip, but decided
for the time being not to make an issue of the matter. He insisted, however, that R. Emmett O'Malley, the insurance superintendent whom Park had
named at Pendergast's dictation, be retained. Governor Stark indicated dissatisfaction with O'Malley, but agreed to keep him "on probation" for a
year.

In November Stark named the Kansas City

Board of Election commissioners and there was not one Pendergast machine man on the board. The boss complained bitterly, accusing the governor of ingratitude, but at the same time arrogantly dismissing Stark and his administration as only a temporary annoyance. "Our organization has carried the state four times," he said, "and it will do so again. Just let the river take its course." It was a remark that he may often have pondered in his cell in Leavenworth prison less than three years later.

The new election board started immediately to clean up the registration lists. By the time it got through it had found approximately 60,000 fraudulent names on the books, and all were stricken off. The purging of the voting lists, wiping out at one stroke 60,000 "sure" votes, was a devastating blow at the source of the Kansas City machine's power. But it was only the first of a series of attacks that were destined to drive the boss completely out of power.

With Pendergast reeling from Governor Stark's blow, but still very much in the ring, another deadly foe jumped into the fight. He was Maurice M. Milligan, then United States District Attorney for the Western District of Missouri.

Three years earlier Milligan's brother, former Representative Jacob L. Milligan, had been a candidate for the Democratic nomination for United States Senator. Pendergast had supported Harry

S. Truman, who won the nomination and the subsequent election and who later became chairman
of the Senate's highly useful and effective "Truman
Committee" for investigation of the war effort.
After the 1934 primary the Milligans uttered loud
but futile cries of fraud, charging that Truman's
nomination had been stolen by means of votes illegally cast or counted by the Pendergast machine.

When the Stark-appointed election board began
going over the padded registration lists and throwing out thousands of names, District Attorney Milligan promptly opened a Federal grand jury investigation of the criminal aspects of the voting frauds
that were being uncovered. There was no lack of
material to work on and no lack of zeal on the
prosecutor's part. Pendergast election judges and
clerks, small but important cogs in the Kansas City
machine, were indicted by the score. All of these
indicted pleaded guilty, were convicted by juries,
or entered pleas of nolo contendere. Some went to
jail. Some went to the penitentiary. Some were
fined. All were punished.

The attack on the machine through prosecution
of its election workers was one arm of a pincers
offensive that Milligan had conceived. Simultaneously he was directing another attack that was
aimed against the boss personally, and which turned
out equally successfully.

Starting in 1922, under a Republican governor,

the state and the stock fire insurance companies had engaged in litigation over rates in Missouri. The litigation continued for many years. It had many angles and time and again one phase or another went to the United States Supreme Court, but by 1932 the court had definitely sustained the state's contention for lower rates.

In one phase of the case $10,000,000 of excess premium payments had been impounded so that it might be returned to the policy holders in the event the state won. The insurance companies, although finally defeated on the rate issue, had no intention of giving up this money. Their whole battery of lawyers was diverted to an effort to salvage the $10,000,000 for the companies rather than let it be returned to the policy holders. Again the insurance companies failed in the courts, after long litigation. Then they worked out a scheme for a "compromise."

Pendergast's insurance superintendent, O'Malley, entered into a secret agreement with the companies, which later became public because of the necessity for confirmation by the courts. Under this agreement the companies were to retain 80 per cent of the impounded money, out of which they would pay attorneys' fees, and the policy holders were to get back only 20 per cent—that is, $8,000,000 for the companies, $2,000,000 for the policy holders.

After this agreement became known Milligan's attention was drawn to it. He could not see how the state officials could have accepted the plan unless somebody had been bribed, and he had a strong suspicion that Pendergast and O'Malley had profited from it. So he turned income tax investigators loose on the job.

Milligan's hunch proved to be a sound one. Boss Pendergast had received a $315,000 bribe from the insurance companies for inducing O'Malley to approve the "compromise" settlement. O'Malley himself, being no "boss," but only a public official who did as he was told, got a mere $62,500 as his own reward for letting the companies get away with $8,000,000.

Both Pendergast and O'Malley had completely forgotten their profitable little deal when they made out their income tax returns the next March 15. Both were convicted of tax evasion in 1939 in the Federal Court in Kansas City. Pendergast went to Leavenworth penitentiary for fifteen months and O'Malley for a year and a day.

Milligan's prosecution of Boss Pendergast seems to have been entirely his own idea, unprompted from Washington. Former Postmaster General and Democratic National Chairman James A. Farley, then at the apex of his political career following President Roosevelt's second election, disapproved heartily of the activities of both Governor Stark and Federal Prosecutor Milligan as tending to weaken the Democratic Party in Missouri. But there was no evidence that he did anything to restrain them. Supreme Court Justice Frank Murphy, who was President Roosevelt's Attorney General at the time, backed up Milligan whenever necessary.

There were other income tax charges against Pendergast, who had forgotten also to report the earnings from some of his private business enterprises. On these, United States District Judge Merrill E. Otis placed him on probation for five years. Under the terms of the probation, the boss was prohibited from taking any part in politics, from even entering his old "state capitol" at 1908 Main Street, and from going outside Kansas City at any time.

Pendergast served his prison term and is now waiting out the period of his probation, living alone in the Ward Parkway mansion that he acquired in the days of his power and crooked money. His wife, who has not lived with him since he was sentenced to the penitentiary, has an apartment in another part of the city.

Milligan had temporarily taken the play away from Governor Stark in the assault on the Pendergast machine, but the governor stepped in after the boss' conviction to deliver the coup de grace to the Kansas City organization. Pendergast and the

machine possibly could have survived the four
years of the Stark administration, the purging of
the voting lists and even the boss' penitentiary sentence, had it not been for the final blow struck by
the governor. That blow wrecked the machine's
control of the Kansas City police department.

Stark was determined that not one vestige of the
machine should remain. He caused to be introduced in the 1939 session of the legislature a bill
to place the Kansas City police department under
a Board of Commissioners appointed by the governor, taking it entirely away from municipal control.

In a memorable legislative fight, the governor's
bill was passed. Pendergast had powerful support
in the legislature, but the governor's aggressiveness
and the weight of public opinion forced favorable
action on the bill. The department was immediately
reorganized. The gambling houses and the vicious
dives were closed, and Kansas City became a vir-
tuous town.

Pendergast had reigned supreme as a boss for
years. He had taken his bribes from insurance companies. As head of the Ready-Mix Concrete Company, he had profited from state, county and municipal highway projects. As head of the Pendergast Wholesale Liquor Company, with strong
leads into the state liquor department, he had seen
to it that virtually every saloon and liquor store

in the state had Pendergast liquor on the shelves, and that they pushed its sale.

But he could not survive honest elections, a penitentiary sentence and an honest police department.

Today the old organization is broken up. Some of its leaders have become active in the "clean up" group, consisting of Democrats and Republicans, which now controls the municipal administration. Possibly some of them are merely marking time, waiting for the day when they can build the old machine back into a semblance of the old organization. But personal jealousies seem to prevent any one of them from making headway.

Old Tom's nephew, young James Pendergast, became the nominal head of the old machine group, but he lacked the force, aptitude and organizing ability of his father or uncle. Frank Shannon, a son of Joe, made a pretense as leader of the remnants of the old Shannon crowd, but with little personal following.

When the Pendergast machine went down, there developed some evidences of the start of a machine in St. Louis to take its place, but it was short-lived. The Democratic mayor, Bernard F. Dickmann, and the chairman of the Democratic City Committee, Robert E. Hannegan, later appointed United States Commissioner of Internal Revenue, started what became known as the Dickmann-Hannegan machine, and made a strong bid for rural support.

For a time it appeared that they would take over control of Democratic politics in the state, but they were too ambitious and tried to build too rapidly. In 1940 they were able to nominate Excise Commissioner Lawrence McDaniel, a Dickmann appointee, for governor. But rural Missouri had just gotten rid of one political machine and it did not want another. The election returns showed McDaniel defeated by his Republican opponent, Forrest C. Donnell, by 3,613 votes.

Then came a scheme typical of political machines. The budding machine leaders in St. Louis met with other Democrats and evolved a plan by which the Democratic legislature would refuse to seat Donnell, and would conduct a partisan legislative investigation of the election through a committee controlled by Democrats. It was expected that the committee would arbitrarily report that McDaniel had been elected and that its report would be approved by the Democratic legislature, which would proceed to install McDaniel in office.

The Republicans appealed to the Missouri Supreme Court, contending that under the law the Speaker of the House of Representatives was required to announce Donnell's election on the face of the returns. All the judges before whom the case was argued were Democrats, but the court upheld the Republican contention. It ordered that

Donnell be seated, leaving McDaniel the right to contest the election under the state statutes, if he desired to do so.

After that the Democrats dropped the scheme, but it had served to wreck the budding Dickmann-Hannegan machine. When Dickmann came up for re-election in the Spring of 1941, just after public sentiment had been aroused to fever heat by the attempted theft of the governorship, he was defeated by a Republican, William Dee Becker, who two years later lost his life in a glider crash at the St. Louis airport.

Hannegan not only survived the episode, but has since proved his political acumen and his administrative ability. In January, 1944 he was elected Chairman of the Democratic National Committee.

In state as well as municipal politics in 1944, Missouri not only had no Democratic boss; it even lacked any recognized leaders. Senator Truman had grown tremendously in national stature since he went to Washington as a Pendergast machine product ten years earlier. But Truman, a mild and modest man, had little inclination for the practical side of politics. He had far more weight in Washington than he had in his home state.

Senator Bennett Champ Clark, who never has forgotten that his father came close to the presidency and who has nourished the secret ambition to succeed where his more able father failed, has more aptitude than his Senate colleague for political connivance. But Clark was so far out on the limb in his opposition to President Roosevelt that he was stymied while Roosevelt remained the party's national leader. Clark faced a fight in 1944 in trying to hold his Senate seat.

III

Missouri's "Golddust Twins" of 1920 have been generally forgotten in the generation of political ups and downs that has intervened since Harding was nominated for President. But they merit at least a brief mention in the story of Missouri machine politics. The "Golddust Twins" became the symbols that marked the end of a fledgling machine which for a few years had controlled Republican destinies in the state.

Principal figures in the dominant Republican group in 1920 were Jacob L. Babler, the national committeeman, Nat Goldstein, a St. Louis committeeman and office holder, and T. W. Hukriede, of Warrenton, who later became a member of Congress.

Before the national assemblage at Chicago which became known as the "smoke-filled-room" convention, there was a lively national contest for delegates between the leading pre-convention can-

didates, Governor Frank O. Lowden of Illinois and
General Leonard Wood. The Lowden managers
obtained the support of the Missouri delegation by
the direct method of sending a sizeable fund of
money into the state and distributing it among influential Republicans.

A United States Senate investigation failed to
track down all of the money to its destination, but
it did disclose that Goldstein and one Bobby Moore
of St. Louis, delegates to the convention, had each
received $2,500 of Lowden money. They became
nationally celebrated as the "Golddust Twins."

This little scandal effectively wrecked what
might have grown into a full-bodied Republican
machine during the GOP decade that followed.
Following the exposure Arthur M. Hyde, later
President Hoover's Secretary of Agriculture, won
the Republican nomination for governor, defeating the machine's candidate, E. E. E. McJimsey,
and the Babler-Goldstein group passed out of the
picture in Missouri politics. Republican politics
became, and have remained, a catch-as-catch-can
affair, with no individual or group ever clearly on
top for long.

During and since the 1940 campaign there has
been some coalescence of Republican groups
around Edgar M. Queeny, wealthy president of
the Monsanto Chemical Company. Queeny was
one of the group of business men who always had

considered themselves above active participation in party politics, but who leaped down into the arena as apostles for the nomination of Wendell L. Willkie for President. Queeny, after 1940, foreswore his support of Willkie and gradually moved over into the extreme anti-Willkie camp. But he apparently liked his 1940 taste of politics, for he remained active in party affairs.

Queeny's influence in the Missouri GOP is easily explained; he has plenty of money and he is willing to contribute generously to the party's campaign chest. Even more than that; he can get a group of wealthy men together at the Racquet Club and, instead of asking for contributions, can tell each of them how much to give.

Missouri's GOP professionals generally have had little confidence in Queeny's ability as a political strategist. They like his money, but override him on political maneuvers. Nevertheless, his influence is real, and it is extensive.

Queeny and his money constitute the principal link between the two strongest factional leaders among the professionals, National Committeeman Barak T. Mattingly of St. Louis and former State Chairman Charles Ferguson, who comes from the Ozark Mountain section of the state. If Queeny succeeds in ironing out the differences between these two, the Queeny-Mattingly-Ferguson trio will form the strongest state-wide group that has existed in the state's Republican organization in a generation.

But, going into the 1944 campaign year, the picture was far from being one of perfect harmony. Governor Forrest C. Donnell was an aspirant for the Republican nomination to run for the Senate against Bennett Champ Clark. So was Howard V. Stephens, St. Louis shoe manufacturer, who was Queeny's choice for the nomination and who had Mattingly's support. And there were other aspirants.

Ferguson was credited with wanting to run for governor, and expected to have Queeny's blessing if he tried it. But Mattingly looked sourly on the prospect of having his party rival in the State House. Whether or not a unified, and therefore effective Republican organization was to emerge seemed to depend on how well the principal factional leaders—with Queeny, and Queeny's money, in the middle—succeeded in working out their rival ambitions.

11

THE KELLY-NASH MACHINE

W
HEN PATRICK A. NASH died on October 6, 1943, Chicago's famous Kelly-Nash Democratic machine became simply the Kelly machine, and it kept right on functioning.

But the machine was showing signs of age. "Pat" Nash or, more often, just "P. A.," was eighty years old at his death. He had been co-boss of Chicago politics since pre-New Deal days. Mayor Edward J. Kelly, the other half of the Kelly-Nash partnership, was sixty-seven years old. And he had no apparent heir as city boss.

The Republicans were growing stronger, having reached a point from which they could hardly have gotten any weaker in the Democratic stronghold on Lake Michigan. They had the help of a recently rewon control of the state government. Mayor Kelly, just re-elected for another four-year term, was safe until 1947, but the Republicans had a chance to get in some body blows if they could cut into the patronage-rich county offices that would be at stake in the 1944 election.

It was by nipping off these county jobs that the Democrats had started the complete overturn of Chicago politics fourteen years earlier. Come what might in national politics, the Kelly machine was prepared to fight with every resource in its power to retain them in 1944.

The Cook County Democratic Central Committee, to give the organization its official title, has boasted, in a formal resolution, of being "the most effective political force in the United States for the promotion of efficient public service and party welfare." Its foes frequently have put it at the head of the list of the "corrupt political machines" which Republican orators like to portray as the chief source of Democratic success in the national field. Actually, the Kelly organization is, by common consent, the strongest political machine in Chicago's history. But it is far from being the most corrupt. Chicago politics set an all-time record for corruption and lawlessness during the lurid decade of the 'twenties, when the city became notorious as the gangster capital of the world. That most of the political scandals of the prohibition and empire-building era involved the Republican city machine and its leaders was attributable only to the circumstance that it was the Republicans who were in power. Both party organizations were equally corrupted by alliances with organized crime on the one hand and with lawless big business on the other. Al Capone and Samuel Insull were real political bosses of the city and of Illinois.

Insull's cynical opinion of public officials and party leaders was that every man had his price. In his savage struggle for economic power he used the leaders of both parties. The public utility empire-builder not only made huge and bi-partisan campaign contributions, he also carried Republican and Democratic leaders, alike, on his list of insiders who were permitted to cash in on Insull stock issues.

At one time he contemptuously proposed to buy the Democratic city machine outright for $500,000 from George E. Brennan, its leader during the 'twenties.

Bombings and gang killings became recognized instruments in political campaigns during the prohibition era. Vote-buying and vote-stealing proceeded on a scale that made latter-day election frauds look like the work of cautious amateurs. The saturnalia of criminal politics reached its climax in the machine-gun killing of William H. McSwiggin, Assistant State's Attorney of Cook County, in 1926, and in the "Pineapple Primary" of 1927, when the explosion of dynamite bombs punctuated a factional fight for control of the Republican party organization.

Killed with McSwiggin were his two companions, one a beer runner and Republican precinct captain, the other a suspected murderer.

The issue in the "Pineapple Primary" was the determination of party control between Chicago's original America First party, headed by Mayor William Hale "Big Bill" Thompson, and the state machine of United States Senator Charles S. Deneen. The homes of Senator Deneen and of Judge John A. Swanson, his candidate for state's attorney, were among those wrecked by bombs.

On "Big Bill's" ticket as candidate for the Republican nomination for governor was former Governor Len Small. During his previous term Governor Small had pardoned eight thousand state convicts in three years, and had himself been indicted on the charge of embezzling $500,000 of public funds during his earlier service as state treasurer. The governor was acquitted but, in a civil suit, was forced to repay $650,000 to the state.

After the governor's acquittal of the criminal charge a grand jury investigated charges that the trial jury had been bribed. Two of the jurors refused to testify and were sentenced to six months in jail for contempt of court. Small commuted their sentences. Three other members of the trial jury subsequently were appointed to state jobs, two as state highway commissioners and one as assistant game warden.

Also on "Big Bill's" machine ticket, as candidate for the nomination of United States Senator, was Colonel Frank L. Smith. He had been elected to the Senate in 1926, but the Senate had refused to seat him after an investigation disclosed that he had spent $458,782 in his campaign, of which $158,000 was contributed by Samuel Insull and $45,000 by other public utility interests. Smith was seeking re-indorsement by the people of Illinois.

In the mayoralty election of the same year, a grand jury investigation later disclosed, "Big Bill" Thompson received a "substantial" campaign contribution from Al Capone, then at the height of his underworld power, and an "advance" of $36,000 from Insull.

Guesses regarding the size of Capone's "substantial" campaign contribution ranged from $100,-000 to as high as $250,000, but the amount never was established officially. The reason was that when a grand jury called Homer K. Galpin, "Big Bill's" campaign manager and chairman of the Cook County Republican Central Committee, to testify regarding campaign contributions, Galpin left town. He hid out for a year and then went to Europe. "On the lam" with him was County Treasurer Harding.

Mayor Thompson's America First-Capone-Insull-Republican city machine was in complete control of Chicago during his term of office. While "Big Bill," the buffoon, was attracting public attention by chasing a phantom King George up alleys, vowing to "punch him in the snoot," the machine was quietly delivering Chicago to the crooks, gamblers and killers, and to the empire-builders of predatory big business.

William E. Dever, an honest judge, was elected as mayor on the Democratic ticket in 1923 and tried to clean up the city. He succeeded only in committing political suicide. "Big Bill," as blatant as ever, came back after a four-year vacation. Dever testified before a United States Senate committee investigating prohibition enforcement that when he assumed office in 1923 "sixty per cent of the police were engaged in the liquor business— not in connivance, but actually." Mayor Dever, running unsuccessfully for re-election in 1927, the year that Capone gave at least $100,000 to the Republican campaign fund, had an offer of a $100,000 contribution from the same source. He refused it, but there was no reason to believe that all Democratic candidates set an equally high standard.

While the Republicans were cashing in the big money from their state and city control, a few Democrats were finding good pickings in lesser offices and less spectacular roles. Two of them were Edward J. Kelly and Patrick A. Nash, the future political rulers of the city. Kelly, in 1920, had become chief engineer of the sanitary district, a separate governmental unit, created by special act of the legislature, whose chief function is the disposal of Chicago's wastes down the Illinois canal. Nash was in the sewer contracting business, which he had inherited from his father, as well as in politics. He had been closely associated politically with Roger Sullivan, Democratic leader of Chicago, and later with George E. Brennan, Sullivan's successor.

Chief Engineer Kelly awarded $8,000,000 in contracts to "P. A.'s" firm, Nash Brothers—and $4,000,000 more to Dowdle Brothers. Dowdle Brothers were "P. A.'s" nephews.

After Kelly became mayor it was disclosed that between 1919 and 1929 his income had been $724,-368, although his salary was only $151,000. Kelly admitted the fact, but never explained it. He paid $105,000 in settlement of Federal income tax claims.

About the same time Nash, who had been listed among Chicago's highest income-earners, also reached a settlement of claims by the government for back income taxes. He paid $175,000 to square his back accounts with Uncle Sam.

That Illinois politics took a clear turn for the better in the early 'thirties was due to the repeal of prohibition and to the desperate financial straits in which the metropolis on Lake Michigan found itself in the depression, rather than to any superior virtue on the part of the Democrats who were just coming into power. What happened, so far as Chicago control was concerned, was that a Democratic spoils machine was substituted for a Republican spoils machine; the city payrolls were purged of Republicans, almost to the last man, and Democrats took their places.

In their public conduct, Governor Horner and Mayor Kelly, the front man of the machine, were regarded generally as improvements over Governor Small, the convicts' friend, and Mayor Thompson, the America First clown who had bankrupted and disgraced the city.

The Democratic machine in Chicago grew up from the saloon meeting days before woman suffrage. It was developed by two Irishmen, Sullivan and Brennan. But in the midland melting pot of Illinois it took a Czech to perfect the machine before it was taken back by the Irish. The Czech was Anton J. Cermak, who was elected mayor in 1931, and who was killed at the side of President-elect Roosevelt in Miami in 1933 by a bullet fired by the assassin, Giuseppi Zangara, and intended for Mr. Roosevelt.

National groups play an important part in Chicago machine politics. The city's population of

3,397,000 in 1940 included 672,000 persons of foreign birth. Of these, 119,000 were born in Poland, 83,000 in Germany, 66,900 in Russia, 66,400 in Italy, 46,000 in Sweden, 40,000 in Ireland, 33,000 in Czechslovakia, 26,000 each in Austria and Lithuania and 13,000 in Greece. The naturalized members of these groups, together with second-generation immigrants, constitute important blocs which are inclined to vote more or less as units. With the exception of the Swedes, who have been generally Republican, and in recent years the Germans and Italians, these groups have formed important segments of the Democratic machine. The Polish, Czech, Lithuanian and Greek nationality groups have received special recognition because of the belief that those groups are highly organized for political action.

It was Cermak's solid Czech following, plus his skill in organizing the other nationality groups, that enabled him to win election as president of the county board, which controls the area of Cook County outside of the Chicago city limits, and thus to spearhead the Democratic return to power in the whole county.

The patronage powers which he acquired with that office enabled him, at the same time, to grab control of the job-hungry Democratic machine from Brennan, whom he proceeded to replace as county leader. An Irish revolt, led by Michael L.

Igoe, was ruthlessly suppressed, and Cermak became the unquestioned boss of the Democratic machine. Igoe, after making his peace with the machine, later was appointed by President Roosevelt as United States District Attorney in Chicago and, finally, as a Federal judge.

Under Cermak's leadership, with the party ticket adequately representing the Jews, the Poles, Czechs, Irish, Italians, organized labor and organized business, the Democrats in 1930 captured the county treasurer's office, the sanitary district board and board of tax assessors, in addition to the county board. Each of these offices carried with it hundreds of patronage jobs.

The following year the Democrats captured City Hall. "Big Bill" Thompson, who had played ball with Al Capone behind his smoke screen of buffoonery, went into the scrap heap. Into his place, as mayor and city boss, stepped "Tony" Cermak, who also had tolerated gang rule in the suburban towns which he controlled, and who was a friend of the liquor interests. On taking office as mayor, Cermak was able to appoint his successor as president of the county board and thus to control both the city and the county governments.

In the 1932 primary the smoothly functioning Cermak machine established its predominant position in the state organization, nominating Henry Horner, a probate judge of good reputation, for governor, and William H. Dieterich for United States Senator. Horner was opposed by "Mike" Igoe, and Dieterich by Scott Lucas, a down-state lawyer who was destined to go to the Senate, but not for another six years.

In the Republican primary, ex-Mayor Thompson's America First machine was making its last-stand fight. Against Senator Otis F. Glenn "Big Bill" ran one Newton Jenkins, who later on was a front man for the Hitlerite German-American Bund in Chicago. Glenn won the nomination with 572,000 votes to Jenkins' 405,000. But the Thompson machine, with its last gasp, carried the governorship primary. In a four-way race, the machine succeeded in nominating former Governor Len Small of malodorous memory.

President Roosevelt carried Illinois by 449,548 votes in November and Dieterich was elected to the Senate by 198,000. But so fearful were the Illinois voters of a return of Len Small to the state house that they supported Horner for governor by a plurality of 566,287, some 117,000 more than the vote for Roosevelt at the head of the ticket.

Small's defeat completely smashed "Big Bill" Thompson's control of the Republican organization. Into his place, as the dominant influence in Illinois Republican affairs, stepped "Colonel" Robert R. McCormick, publisher of the *Chicago Tribune*, the self-styled "world's greatest newspaper."

The *Tribune* had opposed "Big Bill," partly because of the fact that Mayor Thompson had tied himself to Hearst's *Herald-Examiner*, the *Tribune's* morning newspaper rival with which it was in bitter competition. But with Thompson out of the picture, the *Tribune* picked up his nationalistic, anti-British policies where he had left off, and carried on.

The *Tribune's* political power came not only from its dominance of the Illinois newspaper field and its consequent ability to give publicity to its programs and candidates. More important was the practice of Colonel McCormick's newspaper of making ferocious and venomous personal attacks against any public figure with whom the publisher was displeased.

Individuals who aroused McCormick's wrath were hounded relentlessly with "news" stories— angled to get the maximum effect—of their private love lives, if any, of their business transactions and their public actions. Their motives were impugned and their personal deficiencies, real or invented, were spread over the front pages.

It took a courageous man, sure of the spotlessness of his record, to risk the *Tribune's* standard methods of retaliation. Most of the Republican politicians preferred to do Colonel McCormicks' bidding and read nothing but pleasant things about themselves in the "world's greatest newspaper."

The success of this combination of flattery and political assault enabled Colonel McCormick to deliver tangible rewards for those who played the *Tribune's* game. C. Wayland "Curley" Brooks, McCormick's darling because of his successful prosecution of the alleged gang slayer of *Tribune* reporter Jake Lingle, began a notable career as a *Tribune* agent in Illinois politics in 1932 by being nominated—and defeated—for state treasurer.

Cermak, the new city boss, had been guilty of a serious error of judgment at the Democratic national convention, when he allied himself with Tammany boss John Curry and Jersey City's Frank Hague in the "stop Roosevelt" block of big-city bosses which formed around "Al" Smith.

But, like Hague (and unlike Tammany, which continued to sulk), the Chicago boss was quick to jump on the Roosevelt bandwagon after the convention. And with Roosevelt elected, Cermak promptly got in line for his cut in federal patronage and for Chicago's badly needed share of federal relief funds. He was in Miami to talk with James A. Farley and the President-elect about prospective appointments when he was hit by the bullet intended for Roosevelt. ("I'm glad it was me instead of you," he said, as Mr. Roosevelt bent over his hospital bed a few hours later.)

The death of Cermak came at a time when years of misrule had caught up with the Chicago city administration. Taxes were uncollected; unpaid city employes were howling, and the teachers were organizing parades to City Hall. It was just before the bank holiday.

"Pat" Nash, whom Cermak had made chairman of the Cook County Democratic Central Committee, was the logical successor. But "P. A." already was seventy years old. He selected Kelly, the chief engineer of the sanitary district, and the man with whom he had maintained eminently satisfactory business dealings, to take over the mayor's office. The Irish were in the saddle once more.

Kelly's elevation to the mayoralty created a rather delicate situation for him and for Colonel McCormick. The two were old friends. Fifteen years earlier the *Tribune's* publisher had been instrumental in having Kelly appointed chief engineer of the sanitary district, of which McCormick was a former chairman. Their friendship had continued.

It was not broken by Kelly's sudden emergence as Democratic co-boss of the city. McCormick had played both sides of the street before. He simply lost most of his interest in city elections, turning his attention to the national scene and the effort to get "that man" out of the White House. The intensely partisan *Tribune* has never attacked Kelly. And it usually has been able to get what it wanted from the city administration.

The Democratic sweep continued during the

next three years, toppling into the machine's hands virtually all of the rich store of city, county and state patronage jobs once held by the Republican machine.

In 1934 "Mike" Igoe, having returned to the fold, was elected as congressman-at-large. His opponent, beaten by 250,000 votes, was the *Tribune's* "Curley" Brooks. At the same time John Stelle, a prominent legionnaire who figured in a Democratic machine split later on, was elected by the machine to the office of state treasurer.

Mayor Kelly was re-elected in 1935 by the all-time Chicago majority of 631,579 votes over Emil C. Wetten, a weak candidate put up by a weak Republican leadership. There was plenty of inferential basis for the widely held belief that the whole campaign was a sellout by the GOP city organization, arranged by Colonel McCormick and the *Tribune*.

Kelly got 800,000 votes and used the figure as his automobile license number for several years until he moved to 209 Lake Shore Drive, overlooking the lake. Since then his license number has been "209."

By 1936 Mayor Kelly and County Chairman Nash had brought the Chicago machine to a state of near perfection. Out of a total potential Cook County vote of about 1,900,000, it could deliver between 400,000 and 500,000 straight machine votes either in a general election or, what was more important, in a primary contest in which party control was at stake.

The figure has remained about static since then. Kelly's own recent estimate of the machine-controlled vote was 500,000, but 400,000 is perhaps closer to the mark. This means that in an election which brings out the maximum number of voters the machine can deliver approximately 25 per cent of the electorate in a bloc of straight machine votes. (Illinois ballots provide a square in which the voter may indicate his vote for the straight party ticket.)

In off-year elections, when the vote falls as low as 1,200,000, the machine's controlled vote accounts for fully one-third of the total.

The most recent election which showed the true machine strength was a judicial election, which attracted little public interest, in the Fall of 1941. Disregarding the split ballots, the Democrats polled 424,000 straight votes. The Republicans, using their shopworn appeal to the public to rise up and smite the machine, polled 202,000 straight votes— their own machine votes.

The Democratic primary vote in Cook County runs to a top of 900,000 to 950,000, so that in this arena the Kelly machine starts off with approximately half the vote sewed up, in addition to whatever share its candidates may get of the independent Democratic vote.

Although the Kelly-Nash machine, starting in 1936, suffered some setbacks in the nomination of candidates for state office, it never has been beaten on its home grounds in Cook County except by one man, County Judge Edmund K. Jarecki, whose popularity with the big Polish population has enabled him to defy the machine on several occasions. Jarecki's independence has been a nuisance to the machine, since he controls the election machinery of the county. But the machine has found a way to make use even of this circumstance. When it is accused of election frauds the standard reply of the organization's orators has been that the election machinery is in the hands of an opposing faction.

And in recent years the machine has been able to put up a similar defense against the frequently made charges of corruption and alliances with gamblers; for the state's attorney's office, too, has belonged to an in-and-out opponent of the machine, Thomas J. Courtney, who joined Judge Jarecki in bolting to Governor Horner's state house wing of the party in 1936.

Actually, both vote-stealing and venal alliances with gamblers exist within the machine, but they exist at the ward or precinct level rather than on a city-wide basis.

Chicago is divided into fifty wards, each with its local machine boss in the person of a ward leader, or committeeman, who frequently is the alderman. If he is not the alderman, he holds some appointive job. Albert J. Horan, the No. 2 man to Kelly in the machine, is bailiff of the municipal court. Joseph L. Gill, secretary of the city committee, is clerk of the municipal court. Both positions carry with them control over numerous leader patronage jobs.

The ward committeemen, technically, are elected in the primary. In practice, they virtually are appointed by the city bosses. Doorbell-pushing and personal contact with the voters is highly organized by the precincts, of which there are about 3,800 in the city. In the Kelly machine the precinct captains, nearly all of them payrollers, really work at their job of knowing their voters and seeing to it that those who will vote "right" don't overlook their civic duty. On election day each precinct captain normally receives from the machine $40 or $50 for expenses. And the average captain has from four to ten payrollers in his district on whom he can call for free manpower assistance.

The 30,000 "organization" employes on the city and county payrolls are expected to do their parts. Before every election day the machine stages several huge rallies, purely for the payrollers, in large halls in various sections of the city. Every employe, whether on the civil service list or not, receives a card of admission bearing his name. These cards are collected at the door, so that both the department heads and the machine leaders can check up on whether or not any individual employe put in an appearance. The candidates appear at the rallies and make pep talks, similar in purpose to that of a football coach to his team before it takes the field. (The Republican city machine in Philadelphia uses the same system to make sure that the pay-rollers do their part on election day.)

Before the war the Kelly-Nash precinct captains literally played Santa Claus to poor children in their districts. Each child received clothing valued at five dollars, including a dress or trousers, sweater, hat, gloves, stockings, underwear, and an order for a pair of shoes. The clothing was purchased whole-sale under the direction of a committee which included leading Chicago merchants. From 60,000 to 80,000 children received the outfits.

Money for this annual Christmas benefit was raised by a "Night of Stars," an all-night extrava-ganza held in the Chicago stadium, for which the best night club and Hollywood talent was enlisted. "Jimmy" Petrillo, czar of the musicians' union, who is a close friend of Mayor Kelly, cooperated by providing the nation's leading big name bands for the parade of talent. From ticket sales and from the sale of advertising space in a souvenir program (the machine wouldn't miss an obvious one like that) an average of $250,000 a year was raised. Another $125,000 or so for the Christmas fund was produced by an all-city championship football game. In its best and final year, 1941, Mayor Kelly's Christmas campaign fund amounted to $470,000.

The whole Christmas fund project was handled by Corporation Counsel Barnet Hodes, who operates the mayor's "independent" headquarters in election campaigns. Hodes might have been a highly successful advertising man or movie producer if he had not gone in for the law. The campaign "literature" which he produces for Kelly's campaigns is of a very high order of excellence in advertising technique and salesmanship.

Illegal voting, ballot-box stuffing and fraudulent counting exist only on a minor scale in Chicago, particularly since the system of permanent registration, opposed by the machine, was installed in 1936.

Election frauds are confined largely to the poorer, less literate sections of the city. A precinct captain who is caught in any such activity can expect no open aid from the machine, which promptly disavows him.

The Kelly machine has to take a plea, too, on the charge that it is financed, in part, by gambling rings. But, again, the "campaign contributions" and the "protection" which they buy appears to operate on a local, district basis rather than through any city-wide alliance between gamblers and the heads of the machine. The wide prevalence of horse-race betting through hand books, coupled with charges that it exists with the corrupt compliance of the police and the political machine, has been a hot issue in Chicago for years.

The populace of the Windy City, which sheltered the heads of the nation's rum-running syndicates (and voted 699,000 to 69,000 for the repeal of prohibition) seems to feel about "bookies" much as it did about speakeasies. It doesn't see much morally wrong about their activities, but neither does it like to have its police captains muscling in on the rackets.

It might be regarded as a sign of good faith on the part of the city machine that Mayor Kelly has consistently and vigorously sought the passage of a law to legalize and regulate the hand books. Such legislation presumably would eliminate what has been a source of financial support for the district organizations of the machine.

A turning point for the Kelly-Nash machine came in 1936 when steadily worsening relations with Governor Horner, Cermak's man, reached the point at which the Chicago bosses decided to retire him to private life. Governor Horner had offended the machine leaders on patronage matters. But the real reasons for the break were: (1) The governor had vetoed a Kelly-sponsored bill to legalize horse-race betting; and (2) he had put through the legislature on his own accord a bill providing for a system of permanent registration of voters instead of the annual personal registration to which the Chicago machine had accommodated itself.

Kelly picked as the machine candidate for governor Chicago Health Commissioner Herman N. Bundesen, who had a reputation in the city as a vote-getter. After some hesitation Governor Horner entered the primary race for renomination, despite the fact that he, along with everyone else, considered it a hopeless fight.

The campaign was a hot one, enlivened by public washing of dirty linen on both sides. Horner made the most of the traditional antipathy of downstate Illinois to Chicago by directing his fire against the city machine, which he charged with "trying to vote butterflies, fence rails and ghosts." The machine replied with charges that Horner was padding the state payroll in an effort to bolster his own down-state machine. Health Commissioner Bundesen drank acidopholus milk, insisted on having his daily exercise and, at campaign rallies, talked about milk and babies instead of the orthodox campaign topics. As primary day neared it became apparent that Horner was likely to win. In Chicago Judge Jarecki, State's Attorney Courtney and "Al" Horan, who later was to return to the fold and become Kelly's chief lieutenant, bolted the machine to support Horner.

The Kelly machine strained to the limit. On election day the precinct captains were given $100 each, instead of the normal $40 or $50. That made a total of more than $350,000 in "campaign expenses" available to the machine in Chicago alone. An estimated $150,000 was poured into the suburban districts in the rest of Cook County, a total campaign fund of $500,000.

The machine polled 526,116 votes for Bundesen in Cook County, at the rate of approximately a dollar a vote, while Horner, with the backing of some deserters from the machine, received 370,000 votes. Down-state the governor polled 450,000 votes to Bundesen's 133,000.

Horner, to his surprise, had beaten the machine, and shattered its control of state nominations. Peace arrangements were made inside the party and Horner went on to win re-election in November over the *Tribune's* perennial candidate, "Curley" Brooks, who was running for governor that year. Elected as lieutenant governor was John Stelle, a Chicago machine candidate who had survived in the primary.

In 1938 Governor Horner's state-house machine again beat the Chicago machine, winning the United States Senate nomination for Scott Lucas (who had failed to make the grade six years earlier) over Michael L. Igoe. Again Horner's strength was concentrated down-state, where Lucas got

418,530 primary votes to Igoe's 163,999. And again the Kelly machine delivered Cook County, where the vote was 562,000 for Igoe to 383,000 for Lucas.

But Horner had scored one victory over the machine right in its own back yard. Judge Jarecki, whom the bosses had tried to shelve, had Horner's support and won renomination—514,000 to 474,000—over the machine's candidate, Circuit Judge John Prystalski, who had been put up with the hope that he could split Jarecki's Polish vote.

The 1938 campaign marked the emergence of another favorite *Chicago Tribune* candidate, of whom Illinois was to hear more. He was Richard J. Lyons, a fiery orator from Libertyville, Ill., and a long-time member of the state legislature, where he had a reputation for representing the Insull interests. Lyons was nominated, with *Tribune* backing, as Republican candidate for United States Senator. But the Democratic factions had made up after the primary (as they had two years earlier) and Lucas got the full machine vote in Chicago. He defeated Lyons 918,857 to 715,072.

During the height of the Kelly-Nash successes the Republican organization in Chicago, stripped of city, county, state and federal patronage, had fallen to a low ebb. It had been kept alive chiefly by financial and publicity support provided by Colonel McCormick and Chicago's other newspaper "colonel," Frank Knox, publisher of the *Chicago*

Daily News, who ran for vice-president in 1936 on the Republican ticket and four years later became President Roosevelt's Secretary of the Navy.

But after the 1936 Democratic split the GOP began a steady climb in voting power, plugging away at the evils of Democratic machine rule, and profiting by a Mid-Western trend back toward its old Republican allegiance. The instrument of final GOP recapture of the state house in 1940, as it happened, was not Colonel McCormick's personal choice. Dwight Green, a handsome, gray-haired young lawyer, had had a secondary role in the conviction of Al Capone on income tax charges, serving as a special assistant to United States District Attorney George E. Q. Johnson, and later had been appointed by President Hoover as Johnson's successor. Green had remained, somewhat uneasily, in that post until June, 1936, when President Roosevelt and Postmaster General Farley finally got around to selecting a Democrat—"Mike" Igoe—for the job. Thereupon Green had gone back to private practice. His clients, in good Illinois GOP tradition, included some of Chicago's principal public utilities.

Early in the 1939 mayoralty campaign some of the "better elements" of the party, including former Senator Glenn (defeated in 1932), had moved in to try to prevent a repetition of the *Tribune's* suspected sellout of four years earlier. They persuaded Green to run for mayor and were well pleased with the result when he lost to Kelly by only 184,000 votes. But Green failed to make a hit with Colonel McCormick.

The following year, 1940, with the governorship and one seat in the United States Senate at stake, Colonel McCormick played a shrewd game with the public. For weeks the two pet *Tribune* candidates, "Curley" Brooks and Richard J. Lyons, the Libertyville orator, were built up as potential rivals for the nomination for governor. Eventually Brooks declared for senator, and Lyons for governor, which had been the secret plan all along.

Green, too, entered the race for the nomination for governor. The GOP city organization, firmly tied to the *Tribune's* policies, supported Lyons, but Green carried both Cook County and down-state to win the nomination by a margin of 153,000 votes.

The Kelly-Nash machine, in preparing for the 1940 primary, finally conceded what had been demonstrated in 1936 and again in 1938—that it could not successfully buck the down-state anti-machine Democratic vote. At a conference in the executive mansion at Springfield, Nash and the down-state forces controlled by Governor Horner agreed on State Chairman Harry B. Hershey, a close friend of the then gravely ill governor, as the organization candidate to succeed Horner, and on

Senator James M. Slattery, who had been appointed by Horner after the death of Senator James Hamilton Lewis, as the candidate to succeed himself.

Lieutenant Governor John Stelle, who had hoped the machine would pick him for governor, sulked and finally entered the primary as an independent candidate. But the combined Kelly-Nash-Horner forces won with little trouble.

The results firmly established the precedent that in state-wide primary elections the machine could win with down-state candidates, but not with its own purely Chicago machine products.

During the general election campaign, McCormick was overheard talking with society columnist Elsa Maxwell at a performance at the Civic Opera House. The chatter had got around to politics, and the *Tribune's* publisher waxed eloquent about his curly-haired candidate for senator.

"And your candidate for governor, what about him?" the lady asked.

"Oh, yes," said McCormick. "What's his name? Name of a color. Oh, yes, Green. That's it, Green. Just mediocre—just mediocre."

But Green was more than mediocre as a vote-getter.

In November President Roosevelt carried Illinois by a slim majority of 95,694 over Wendell L. Willkie, while Green led the state Republican ticket to victory with an astounding majority of 256,945 votes over Democratic candidate Hershey. The big "swing" occurred in Cook County, where President Roosevelt beat Willkie by 233,000 votes, while Green, the Republican, carried the county by 63,000.

It looked as if the Republicans had sold out Willkie in return for Democratic votes for Green. The old cry of "deal" was raised again but, while the circumstances were suspicious, no out-and-out deal could be proved.

"Curley" Brooks, carried along on the tide, finally won a seat in the Senate by the skimpy but sufficient margin of 20,827 votes.

The only Democratic state victor was Secretary of State Edward J. Hughes. In Illinois secretaries of state are hard to beat. All of them have established large and loyal personal followings through the pleasant and harmless practice of issuing thousands of "special" automobile license numbers to key individuals around the state. Hughes won re-election by a majority of 133,000 votes, topping even the vote for President Roosevelt, and thereby became, automatically, a strong contender for the Democratic nomination for governor in 1944.

Green's election produced a situation, with regard to GOP internal control, which called for some careful handling.

Earlier in the year the *Tribune* had installed

Werner W. Schroeder, a smart, experienced politician, as National Committeeman from Illinois. Green was a novice in practical politics and, while he was not a *Tribune* man, he shared the disinclination of all Illinois politicians for antagonizing that newspaper's vindictive publisher.

A balance of power evolved, in which Green, the amateur, remained titular leader of the state machine while Schroeder, the politician and *Tribune* spokesman, emerged as the dominant influence in the party. In 1942 the *Tribune* backed him for chairman of the Republican National Committee. Wendell L. Willkie, one of the national leaders of the GOP who has been willing to do open battle with Colonel McCormick, prevented his election at the National Committee meeting in St. Louis.

Schroeder is a personal protege of former Governor Len Small, who financed his education at the University of Michigan. When Small was governor, Schroeder had what is perhaps the choice patronage job in the state. He was attorney for the public administrator of Cook County, a fee job which can produce a legitimate "take" for the holder of around $25,000 a year. Since Green has been governor the same job has been held by John T. Dempsey, a Chicago supporter whom Green installed as chairman of the Chicago Republican City Committee.

An embarrassing journalistic faux pas upset the

Tribune's program for the 1943 mayoralty campaign. As candidate for mayor Colonel McCormick had selected Roger Faherty, a wealthy young lawyer whose father, the late Michael Faherty, had been "Big Bill" Thompson's commissioner of public works. But the *Tribune*, confident that its wishes would be observed, made the mistake of announcing the selection of Faherty as the candidate before the Republican City Committee had a chance to act on the matter.

It became so obvious to everyone that the candidate had been hand-picked by the *Tribune*—which as a rule stays modestly behind the scenes in such matters—that the city committee, after several days of conference and much hemming and hawing, persuaded Faherty to withdraw.

Governor Green then put in his own hand-picked candidate, George B. McKibbin, a lawyer and civic worker whom the governor had previously appointed as state director of finance. McKibbin was also the son-in-law of Bernard Edward Sunny, head of the biggest Mid-Western public utility combination since Insull's day.

Among his many other interests Sunny is a director of the Chicago City Railway Company, chairman of the bondholders' protective committee of the Chicago City and Connecting Railways, and a member of the board of operations of the Chicago Surface lines.

Mayor Kelly, in his campaign, made the most of his charge that the Republicans were still under the thumb of the utilities and, specifically, that they planned, through McKibbin and the Green-appointed Illinois Interstate Commerce Commission, to block the mayor's streamlined transit unification plan, which the street railways opposed.

As between the Democratic and Republican machines the voters picked the former, but the majority for the head of the Kelly-Nash machine was only 114,020. The vote was: Kelly 685,567; McKibbin 571,547. The Republicans were creeping up.

Late in September of 1943 a West Side tough known as "Sonny Boy" Quirk was killed in Chicago in good old 1927 style. A short while before one "Danny" Stanton, a gunman who had survived the prohibition wars, had also been killed. It developed that Quirk had moved from the West Side to the South Side to take over the late Mr. Stanton's interests in the hand-book business.

Entirely contrary to Chicago custom, detectives from State's Attorney Courtney's office caught a small-time gangster who "squealed" and named five suspects as the killers of Quirk.

The unprecedented apparent solution of a gangland killing (the suspects later were acquitted) aroused so much excitement that the grand jury's murder probe developed into a full dress investigation of gambling and of the failure of the police to interfere with it. Several police captains were indicted for complicity in the hand-book operations. Lesser policemen were suspended.

It was almost painfully evident to Chicago political insiders that Courtney's clean-up was carefully avoiding the gold coast and the Barbary coast, north of the Loop, and a few other areas in which local police control was in the hands of Courtney's political supporters.

The knowing ones guessed that one of the results of the big police-gambling probe would be an eventual patching up of the old Kelly-Courtney feud, with Courtney being admitted to the inner circle of the machine.

But, meanwhile, the clean-up drive was hitting the Kelly machine both in its pocketbook and in its prestige. And it was providing a new store of ammunition for Republican orators in that approaching 1944 battle for the county offices.

The Republicans were on the upsurge. They had reason to believe that a substantial transfusion of county patronage, if they could grab it, would make the old GOP machine virtually as good as new.

12

SUN-KISSED POLITICS

CALIFORNIA presumably is the place where Philadelphia Democrats and New York, Chicago and Jersey City Republicans go when they die. It is an appropriate heaven for civic reformers. It has no political machines.

The big bosses in California are the lobbyists and pay-off men for the Standard Oil Company, the Townsend Clubs, the Pacific Gas and Electric Company, the League of Women Voters, the Southern Pacific Railroad, the Federation of Women's Clubs, the Bank of America, the State Federation of Labor, the Associated Farmers, and about twenty other recognizable pressure groups. And since each of them frequently is pulling in a direction different from that of all the others, none succeeds for long in being more than a section foreman.

For candidates and office holders, California is not Utopia. It is just plain hell, in which office seekers are pulled and tugged out of shape and bombarded with threats, promises and bribes. Small wonder that some of them become so confused that they have no idea how they got elected and wind up by being grateful to the wrong people.

Back at the beginning of the century California politics was ruled by a corrupt Republican machine, centered in San Francisco, which was owned body and soul by the Southern Pacific Railroad. Railroad attorneys openly ran the party conventions, the state legislature and the chief executive's office. The bar of the Palace Hotel in San Francisco was the real state capitol. As one of the railroad's minor courtesies, round trip tickets from Sacramento to San Francisco were placed on each legislator's desk every week-end. Hotel bills were sent directly to the railroad company.

Street railway and telephone franchises and all similar city and state favors to the public utility companies were on sale to the highest bidder. Gas rates could be raised by the Pacific Gas and Electric Company in return for a $20,000 lump payment and a $1,000 a month retainer for San Francisco boss Abe Ruef.

That regime, more brazen if not more corrupt than similar ones of the period in other states, was broken up in a series of prosecutions in 1906 and

1907. Special prosecutor Francis J. Heney, who began the investigation, was shot down in the court room by a would-be assassin. Hiram W. Johnson, his assistant, carried on with sufficient success to make it certain that a grateful California electorate would keep him in public office—as governor and United States Senator—from then on.

While Johnson was governor a sweeping series of governmental reforms was adopted. In its wide open primaries and in the initiative, referendum and recall provisions of its constitution, California offers unsurpassed instruments for direct government by the people. But not even Hiram Johnson at his peak could devise a law that would guarantee adequate leadership to the voters in the use of those instruments.

As the wave of reform passed, the big business groups, well supplied with slush funds, began to worm their way back into the governmental setup. The Southern Pacific's monopoly had been broken; but a dozen big companies soon were exercising, combined, almost as great influence. The Republican machine was crushed; but the principal campaign contributors found compensating advantages in dealing directly with the candidates instead of through an intermediary.

Methods changed. The modern technique of advertising and propaganda began to supplement bribes as the chief means of political control. Candidates with no organized backing had to sell themselves to the voters as they would have sold a new mouthwash or deodorant. That took money, and plenty of it. And California's business interests still had plenty of money to spend in buying the good will of legislators and local officials.

At the state capitol in Sacramento campaign contributions were handed out by the lobbyists, who were also on hand during the sessions to advise the recipients of such largesse on their votes. The state legislature became—and remains—one of the most lobby-ridden in the world.

California got along, until 1932, without any Democratic Party. There were Democratic voters, as there were Socialist and Prohibitionist voters. And there were enough independents to carry the state for Woodrow Wilson in 1916 by a plurality of 3,806 votes and thus make possible his re-election as President. That year the Socialist candidate for President received 43,250 votes in California, and the Prohibition Party's candidate received 27,689 votes.

In 1924 the presidential race in California was between President Coolidge, who received 733,250 votes, and Senator Robert M. LaFollette, Progressive Party candidate, who polled 424,649. The Democratic Party had virtually disappeared. Its candidate for President, John W. Davis, got a mere 105,514 votes, about eight per cent of the total.

There was not the vestige of a working Democratic organization in the state. Former Secretary of the Treasury William Gibbs McAdoo and publisher William Randolph Hearst were able to manipulate the state delegations to the party's national conventions, the only phase of party affairs which retained any importance.

The election machinery and all state offices were firmly in the hands of the Republicans.

Guiding influences of the Republican organization were the state's big oil, railroad and public utility interests, speaking through the kindred voices of Harry Chandler, publisher of the *Los Angeles Times*, George T. Cameron, publisher of the *San Francisco Chronicle*, and Joseph Knowland, publisher of the *Oakland Tribune*. The endorsement of the "Chandler-Knowland-Cameron axis," as it is known in California, became recognized as a sine qua non for nomination for a statewide elective office in the Republican primary.

The depression of 1930 and 1931 hit California particularly hard, especially the southern portion around Los Angeles, the political pivot of the state. It caused a political revolution.

President Roosevelt's success in carrying the state in the 1932 election was the result of a statewide uprising against the party in power. But it was a spontaneous and unorganized uprising. Along with Mr. Roosevelt, it swept the veteran McAdoo into office as a member of the United States Senate.

The people of California were up in arms, but they constituted a mob rather than an army. What they needed was a leader who could crystallize the sentiment for revolt into a unified political force. The leader arose in the person of Upton Sinclair, the socialist novelist and several times Socialist candidate for governor. Sinclair wrote one of his persuasive pamphlets in which he advocated a method of production for use instead of the existing system of curtailment of production for profit. The pamphlet was entitled "End Poverty in California." Around its author a strange political organization crystallized. Taking its name from the initials of Sinclair's pamphlet, the movement which he headed called itself the EPIC movement. It stormed the Democratic primaries in overwhelming force and won for Sinclair the Democratic nomination for governor over the futile opposition of the traditional "McAdoo Democrats."

The campaign which followed was weird and unprecedented.

Los Angeles for years had been a city of many strange religious sects and of radical and unorthodox types of organizations. The desperation of the times coalesced all of them into one great surging political movement which, with little money, but with tremendous enthusiasm, entered into the campaign to make Sinclair the governor of California.

Economic conditions were ripe for the crusade. There were hundreds of thousands of destitute people. They, and thousands of others barely better off, could see mountainous piles of agricultural products from the rich California soil being destroyed because there was no profitable market for them. Vast crops of oranges were covered with kerosene and burned. In the truck garden fields huge piles of onions, carrots and potatoes were similarly destroyed.

The unorthodox EPIC movement gathered a momentum which seemed likely to sweep Sinclair into the governership. Terrified, but not paralyzed, by the prospect, the industrial powers that be threw everything they had into the fight to kill off the Socialist pamphleteer and to re-elect safe, sound and conservative Governor Merriam.

How much money was poured into the campaign never will be known with exactness. Only a fraction of it passed through the hands of the Republican campaign committee. Most of it was spent directly by the financial and industrial interests which sprang openly into the fight.

One California official has fixed $10,000,000 as a conservative estimate of the total amount spent to re-elect Governor Merriam. It could hardly have been less. One year later the chain retail stores alone spent $1,142,033 in a referendum campaign to defeat a proposed tax on chain stores. And the chain stores are insignificant by comparison with the concentrated wealth and power of the interests which were massed against Sinclair.

They plastered every billboard in the state with anti-EPIC posters and slogans. They used payroll slips, form letters, and paid as well for plenty of free newspaper space to convince their employes that quick and inevitable personal and individual disaster would follow if Sinclair were elected as governor. Industries, singly and in groups, threatened to close up or move out of the state. Teachers and other public employes were warned of payless pay days under government by the impractical Sinclair and his horde of crackpot supporters. On election day the banks, insurance companies and other public institutions closed their doors and sent their frightened employes out to vote against Sinclair.

For the first time in a generation there were charges of vote stealing and fraudulent counting of the returns, one of the typical evils of machine rule from which California, before and since, has happily been free. It is possible that the count was fraudulent. Sinclair's foes had stopped at nothing else. The Republicans were in charge at all of the polling places. The EPIC watchers, where there were any, were rank amateurs.

With it all, Sinclair came within 100,000 votes

of being elected—a narrow squeak for the conservative rulers of the state.

The EPIC campaign failed to elect a governor, but it did produce a Democratic party in California for the first time. The 1932 campaign had created the raw material for an opposition party. The EPIC campaign two years later solidified this raw material into a powerful political force out of which evolved a party machinery and a party personnel. And it laid the basis for subsequent party victory.

The old-line Democrats, including McAdoo, National Committeeman Isidore Dockweiler and National Committeewoman Lucretia Del Vai Grady, had opposed Sinclair. The new party members lumped them all under the disapproving term "McAdoo Democrats," and looked on them with deep suspicion for years afterward.

The Sinclair uprising had elected numerous local officials, and thirty-seven EPIC-Democratic members to the state legislature. These became the backbone of the new Democratic Party. One of them was Culbert L. Olson, a Los Angeles lawyer, who was elected to the state Senate, and who proceeded to upset the normal routine of that body.

Olson picked as his special dragon the Standard Oil Company of Southern California, one of the recognized powers behind the Republican organization. At the time the Standard Oil Company was backing a referendum on what was known as the Sharkey bill, a measure providing for control of oil production by a state commission. Opponents contended that the measure also was designed to give the Standard Oil Company, in practice, control of the proposed commission. Olson led the fight against the Sharkey bill and it was defeated by a large majority.

Another campaign which he launched, and successfully carried through, forced the oil company to make restitution to the state for oil which it had obtained by drilling "slant wells" from its property under oil lands owned by the state.

The dragon was not slain—apparently it was only slightly inconvenienced and annoyed—but the fight promoted Olson into such a position of state-wide prominence that he became a natural successor to Upton Sinclair, now retired to his writing, as leader of the curious conglomeration that made up the new Democratic Party. He became a candidate for governor.

McAdoo's term in the Senate was running out, and it was a foregone conclusion that no genuine EPIC would vote to send him back there. He had been elected on President Roosevelt's coat tails, with only a meager organization, and while in the Senate he had had no close liaison with the folks back home. He was regarded as being as much a resident of New York as of California.

Sheridan Downey had been the candidate for lieutenant governor on Sinclair's EPIC ticket. Subsequently he had become the champion of all of the numerous and powerful old-age pension organizations in the state. He became a natural candidate for McAdoo's Senate seat.

The same forces that had supported Sinclair, much better organized and supplemented by a new crop of Southern California panacea groups, pitched into the 1938 battle. Olson was elected as governor and Downey as senator, in the first Democratic victory in a state election in the memory of the oldest resident.

A description of the mechanics by which this success was obtained will show the Democratic Party of California in action.

An important element in the Olson-Downey victory was the enthusiastic support which they received from the Townsend Clubs, a political action group which has lost none of its influence in the state of its birth. The clubs were organized to support the $200-a-month old-age pension plan originated by Dr. Francis E. Townsend, a Long Beach, California, physician. Their political program later became much broader, although pensions remained the cardinal point. During periods of political lull, the clubs carry on a social existence. The old folk who comprise their membership meet weekly, sing hymns and otherwise entertain

themselves. Many of the clubs are headed by retired ministers.

As election time approaches the character of the
Townsend clubs undergoes a complete change.
They spring into action on behalf of candidates—
of either party—who meet their primary test by
promising to support increased old-age pensions.
If all of the candidates are whole-hearted pension
advocates, as often happens in areas where the clubs
are particularly strong, the Townsendites weigh
other factors in deciding whom to support. Their
support is effective and their enmity dangerous.

In the Downey-Olson campaign, in fashion that
has since become standard, the old folk canvassed
their neighborhoods on a door to door basis, taking
the place of precinct workers in a well organized
political machine. They prepared circulars, collected money, addressed envelopes and helped in
rounding up the voters and getting them to the
polls on election day.

Few California politicians, since 1938, have been
known as opponents of bigger and better pensions.
The Ham-and-Eggs societies, with their slogan of
"Thirty Dollars Every Thursday," were a similarly
active factor in California in the 'thirties. With no
jobs and nothing to occupy their time, the "Thirty
Dollars Every Thursday" advocates held mass
meetings, organized, prepared literature which was
distributed from door to door by volunteer work-

ers, and made themselves felt in political campaigns.

Another organization which was extremely active at the time was the Utopian Movement. It was a secret society, which swept rapidly through Southern California by means of a chain-letter membership drive. Every new member was expected to organize his neighborhood and get several new members. A prospect would be invited by word of mouth to attend a neighborhood meeting where, with all the trappings of robes, masks and weird lights, he would see a playlet which was designed to teach the economic lesson that there should not be hunger in the midst of plenty. At one time 10,000 members attended a meeting of the Utopian Movement in the Shrine auditorium in Los Angeles.

The Utopians, too, pitched into the Olson-Downey campaign, with noticeably efficient effect.

Labor unions contributed in money and campaign manpower, as well as in votes, to the victory. In California's political vacuum (so far as political organizations are concerned) organized labor plays a more important part than it does in many other states.

Helen Gahagan, actress wife of Melvyn Douglas, and the Democratic National Committeewoman from California, had a star role in the campaign. Miss Gahagan's political importance, which is great, does not come directly from her party position. Her chief function in California campaigns is to serve as a connecting link between the candidates and the state's numerous politically important women's organizations. Chief of these are the League of Women Voters, the American Association of University Women, the Business and Professional Women's clubs and the California Federation of Women's Clubs.

It was a conglomeration of such clubs, societies, movements, organizations, associations and leagues and their members which accounted for the Democratic victory.

On the other side there was a not dissimilar conglomeration of special interests backing the Republican candidates. They had more money, but fewer members and fewer votes. Among them were the chambers of commerce, manufacturers' associations, the Associated Farmers, formed to prevent the unionization of farm laborers, various employer organizations and the individual corporation which had discovered the method of getting along with California Republicans, and weren't too sure how they would make out with the untried Democrats.

In the 1942 campaign, in which Governor Olson was defeated for re-election by Attorney General Earl Warren, the Republican candidate, the general line-up was similar. That the result was different was due to several factors.

President Roosevelt and his political aides in the national administration, perhaps guided by Mc-Adoo, never had given a cordial welcome to the EPIC-Townsend brand of Democracy which had taken over the party label in California.

During the third term campaign in 1940 Edward J. Flynn, chairman of the National Committee, entrusted the management of the far western campaign to Edwin P. Pauley, who, up to that time, never had been a figure in politics. Pauley, with his father, was the owner of the Petrol Oil Company, an "independent" oil-producing concern. But many apparently independent oil companies in California operate under the control of the Standard Oil Company.

When Pauley leaped suddenly into political prominence after collecting $50,000 in campaign contributions, some of the California Democrats of EPIC origin raised their eyebrows ever so slightly. And when Pauley was appointed secretary and acting treasurer of the Democratic National Committee, and introduced by Flynn to a group of California congressmen as "a good man to know," the new Democrats in the sunny land of utopias began to wonder whether or not somebody was selling them down the river to the old enemy.

Governor Olson himself had sacrificed some of his popularity as a crusader against the wicked

Standard Oil Company by his favorable reception of an oil-control bill introduced by Maurice Atkinson, an assemblyman from Long Beach. The independent oil producers regarded the Atkinson bill as containing all of the bad features of the Sharkey bill, against which Olson had crusaded. And as background for this development, there were the rumors that the bi-partisan Standard Oil Company had played it safe by contributing to Olson's campaign fund, as well as to that of his GOP opponent, in 1938.

All in all, many of California's new Democrats were more than slightly cool toward the national party and toward Governor Olson by the time he ran for re-election. Their choice as a candidate would have been Robert W. Kenny, the president of the National Lawyers Guild, who eventually wound up on the ticket as the candidate for Warren's old job as attorney general. Kenny's election to that office, and the defeat of the rest of the ticket, established him as the new party leader.

More important than these elements of Democratic weakness were the positive tactics adopted by the Republicans.

Close study of the previous election results had convinced the smarter back-stage Republican managers that commercial salesmanship was the key to the California election riddle. In the 1942 campaign the best brains of the advertising and sales departments of California's big industries were assigned to the task of offering the California voters what they wanted.

Earl Warren was a sure-fire cleaner which wouldn't stain your most delicate fabrics. He was a mouthwash which would remove every trace of unpleasant breath. He was a bath soap which would leave you dainty and proof against any hint of body odor. Satisfaction guaranteed, or double your money back.

He sounded good to California, and the people bought him.

The biggest obstacle to the formation of an effective and responsible Democratic Party organization out of the majorities which Democratic candidates amassed in the presidential and congressional elections in the decade starting in 1932 and in the state election of 1938 has been the provisions of the election law governing the open primaries.

Any person with ten dollars to spare can file as a candidate for any office he wants and have his name appear on the ballot along with all the other candidates. And under the peculiar California practice of cross filing, if he has another ten dollars, and five friends in the opposition party to sign his entry papers, he can become a candidate in that party's primary, too.

The first principle of party government is that a

party shall be able to select its candidate freely and match him against the other party's freely chosen candidate. In California it doesn't work that way. Cross-filing is a device by which the candidate of the minority party—at present the Republicans—can attempt, and often successfully, to beat the game.

If five Democrats are seeking the party nomination for an elective office, not an extraordinary situation, the Republican candidate can enter the Democratic primary as a sixth candidate, and, what with the loose party affiliations that exist in California, stand a good chance of winning the Democratic nomination as well as his own party's and having no major party opposition in the general election.

This has become almost standard procedure in California elections.

To make matters worse, the state and county committees of both parties are prohibited by their rules from endorsing any primary candidate or designating any of the primary entries as the choice of the party organization. The Republicans, with an older organization and better party discipline, frequently are able to arrange things so that only one party candidate is entered for each office. In the past few years the Democrats have attempted to apply pressure to the same end through "rump" committees having no official standing.

If both parties succeed in this effort the result is that the field is limited to one Democratic and one Republican candidate for an office. Each of these is then entered in both party primaries. Assuming that each wins his own party's nomination, they can then fight it out in the general election. The effect of this system is to nullify completely the intent of the party primaries.

California, to the outsider, presents a picture of pressure politics gone wild. But the picture makes sense to Arthur Samish, kingpin of the lobbyists who gather at the state capitol in Sacramento. The lobbyists know what they want and they usually know how to get it.

Samish represents the liquor interests and serves as an intermediary between the representatives of the people and many of California's other special interests. He can get a legislator a campaign contribution from almost any source that may be desired.

And the picture makes sense, too, to the Messrs. Chandler, Cameron and Knowland who, through the influence of their newspapers, are able to select Republican candidates for state office.

13

THE "REALIST"

THE FACT THAT a national administration dedicated to the highest principles of liberalism and
progressive democracy is found to be working
hand-in-glove with political machines of questionable morals, at best, is hardly a matter for
surprise.

President Roosevelt, not so long ago, impishly
linked himself with Russia's Marshal Stalin as a
"realist." And, despite all that has been said in
praise and in denunciation of the "idealism" of the
New Deal, it is a fact that the Roosevelt administration always has had its feet firmly planted in
the realities of practical politics.

If, therefore, it follows that the feet must be of
clay, that is a conclusion which arises from the
nature of American politics rather than from the
weaknesses of any particular politician. No public
official who neglected the realities represented by

precinct workers, ward leaders, city and state bosses, would ever be likely to write any record of great accomplishments in public life in the present stage of American democracy.

The relation between the Roosevelt administration and the big-city Democratic machines is an aspect of national politics which can more easily be distorted by over-emphasis than by complete silence. Voting frauds, sale of public offices, grafting on contracts and the existence of alliances with the criminal underworld are among the political realities of America. But they are almost entirely local in character. They did not originate with the New Deal, and they never have been confined to one party.

President Roosevelt, as a realist, has followed normal political practice in exchanging mutual aid with those machines which supported him and his political program, and in fighting those which opposed him.

Governor Thomas E. Dewey, scourge of the New York Democratic machines, has followed exactly the same policy. The Republican machines which Dewey has aided with patronage have morals that in general are indistinguishable from those of their Democratic counterparts in the Empire State. And Dewey's feud with the Syracuse Republican organization headed by former Mayor Rolland B. Marvin—who has aligned himself with

Wendell L. Willkie—is exactly comparable to President Roosevelt's long quarrel with Tammany Hall when it sided against him with "Al" Smith.

It is a mistake to suppose that Mr. Roosevelt ever has been dependent on the big-city bosses for his own election to the office of President. He won the nomination in 1932 over the determined opposition of the bossed convention delegations, including those from New York City, Jersey City and Chicago.

After the convention Frank Hague and Chicago's Mayor Cermak hurriedly ate the unkind words they had said about the candidate, and were welcomed aboard the Roosevelt bandwagon. The bosses, being realists, were merely protecting themselves. They knew that Mr. Roosevelt would be elected with or without their support, and it is one of the first principles of realistic politics to try to be on the side of the winner.

Boss Kelly, Boss Hague and Boss Crump led the "draft Roosevelt" movement in 1940, and are leading it in 1944, for a very realistic reason. They were convinced, and are convinced, that he is the strongest possible Democratic candidate. His nomination in 1944 means to them not only the best opportunity of continuing to share in Federal patronage, but also the best method of strengthening their local tickets. President Roosevelt could contribute more to the election of Democratic county officials in Chicago in 1944 than the Kelly machine could contribute to the re-election of the President for a fourth term.

While the machines have not been necessary for the President's own elections, they have played an important part in the accomplishment of his political purposes. The disciplined, machine-controlled delegations have been his front-line troops in party conventions and in Congress. At the 1940 national convention they helped bring about the nomination of Henry Wallace for Vice-President, and they will provide disciplined support for the President's program at the 1944 convention. In Congress, the bossed delegations from Brooklyn, the Bronx, Tammany Hall (at times), Chicago and New Jersey, have been strong nuclei of support for the foreign and domestic policies of the administration.

When Tammany's Boss Curry continued to sulk after Mr. Roosevelt's nomination and election in 1932, the President promptly declared war on Tammany Hall. His objective, as in the war against the Axis, was unconditional surrender. But Mr. Roosevelt never had any thought of destroying Tammany, or dismembering it. As a realist, what he wanted was to have control of Tammany put in friendly hands. And when he obtained that with the election of "Mike" Kennedy as Tammany leader in 1942, the President came through handsomely with patronage appointments designed to bolster Kennedy's leadership.

There is nothing abstract about the President's understanding with Frank Hague and "Ed" Kelly. Both have given powerful and undeviating support to the President, his candidates and his legislative policies. In return, the President has accepted their recommendations in the appointment of federal judges, prosecutors, marshals and collectors of internal revenue and customs.

And that, in a nut shell, is the American system of practical politics.

It is a system that is violated only under extreme provocation and usually with suicidal results. Tom Pendergast and Boss Hague provided the extreme provocation in their arrogant claims to supreme power in their respective states. Governor Lloyd C. Stark of Missouri completely crushed the Pendergast machine, but, while Pendergast went to the penitentiary, Governor Stark went back to private life and the Republicans took over the state government.

Governor Charles Edison failed to administer the coup de grace to Hagueism, but the main beneficiaries of their three-year fight were the Republicans, who recaptured the state government. Hague was weakened and Edison eliminated, at least temporarily, as a major political factor in the state.

Are the big-city political machines "reactionary," as Wendell Willkie has called them? Obviously, they are in their local practices. But in national affairs it is another story.

In a democratic political system the mere existence of a "boss," with individual power to name
candidates and to determine policies, is patently
"reactionary." The boss system, in Republican
Philadelphia and Buffalo, as well as in Democratic
New York, Chicago, Memphis and Jersey City,
makes a mockery of the supposed right of the
voters to choose their local public officials. Judges,
congressmen, sheriffs, mayors and governors who
have been hand-picked by a political boss acknowledge a responsibility to the boss rather than to the
people as a whole.

Yet Alfred E. Smith, in his day, was a great
American liberal. Under his leadership New York
set the pace for the country in the enactment of
enlightened labor and social legislation. "Al" Smith
was a product of Tammany Hall and, as a realist,
he never forgot that his power depended on main-
taining the support of Tammany Hall and of the
other machines which controlled the Democratic
Party in New York State.

If Sheriff Thomas M. "Tin-Box-Tom" Farley
was salting away a fortune whose origin he could
not satisfactorily explain, and district leaders were
selling appointments to the city magistrate's court

at $10,000 each, this was perhaps offset by the fact that the Tammany delegation at Albany was helping to place on the statute books the nation's most advanced factory inspection laws, workmen's compensation laws, and measures to protect the state's natural resources from exploitation by predatory private interests.

Another Tammanyite of the Smith and "Charlie" Murphy era is United States Senator Robert F. Wagner, who has given his name to the Social Security Act and to the National Labor Relations Act. No respectable "reactionary" would admit any spiritual kinship to Wagner or to any of his acts.

"Dictator" Hague's personal representative in Congress is Mrs. Mary T. Norton, chairman of the House Committee on Labor. While Hague's police, prosecutors and judges were driving CIO representatives out of Jersey City, Mrs. Norton was leading the fight for the Wages and Hours Bill, and was making her committee a burying ground for anti-labor legislative proposals of all sorts.

The House contains no more militant "liberal" than Representative Adolph J. Sabath, of Chicago, the chairman of the Rules Committee, who owes his position in Congress entirely to the favor of Boss Kelly.

These are not merely isolated examples. In general it can be said that the bossed delegations from the nation's big cities have provided the most consistent and effective support for the "liberal" domestic program of the New Deal and, usually, for the administration's foreign policy as well.

Within the Democratic Party the outstanding "reactionaries" have come from the states where no effective party machine operates and where it is a case of every demagogue for himself. Excellent examples of this are Senator W. Lee "Pass-the-Biscuits-Pappy" O'Daniel, from the unbossed state of Texas, and Senator Theodore "The Man" Bilbo, from the equally unbossed state of Mississippi. Both of them served as governors of their states before being elected, without the aid of party bosses, to the United States Senate.

So it appears that while the machines are "reactionary" in local affairs, the public officials whom they produce and keep in office in Washington usually are not. The explanation lies in the fact that the big-city bosses, like all dictators, can maintain their power indefinitely only by giving their subjects a good measure of what they want from government.

As long as a machine produces front men of the calibre of "Al" Smith and "Bob" Wagner, provides a certain amount of progressive legislation for the benefit of the whole people, and serves as a buffer between the needs of the ignorant and the complexities of government, it can safely get away with a certain amount of private graft and corruption.

And as long as Bosses Hague, Kelly, Pew and Jaeckle control important portions of the political organizations of their respective parties, it may be taken for granted that the candidates of both parties for all offices, up to and including that of President, will seek their support and will offer suitable rewards in the way of spoils after they are elected.

That is "realism" in American politics in 1944.